Pitching With Tom Seaver

PITCHING WITH TOM SEAVER

by Tom Seaver
with Steve Jacobson

Prentice-Hall, Inc.

Englewood Cliffs, N.J.

Pitching with Tom Seaver by
Tom Seaver with Steve Jacobson

Printed in the United States of America
10 9 8 7 6 5 4 3 2 1

Prentice-Hall International, Inc., London
Prentice-Hall of Australia, Pty. Ltd., North Sydney
Prentice-Hall of Canada, Ltd., Toronto
Prentice-Hall of India Private Ltd., New Delhi
Prentice-Hall of Japan, Inc., Tokyo

Library of Congress Cataloging in Publication Data

Seaver, Tom,
Pitching with Tom Seaver.

SUMMARY: Tips on effective pitching technique by a
pitcher considered one of the best in the major leagues.
I. Pitching (Baseball)—Juvenile literature.
II. Pitching (Baseball)] I. Jacobson, Steve.
II. Title
GV871.S4   796.357.22   73-8992
ISBN 0-13-676981-0

Contents

1

Why Be a Pitcher?

Save yourself a lot of hard work for a lot of years. Don't be a pitcher. It's too hard, too much work, too much trouble. Other positions — even other sports — are a lot easier. Why would you want to be a pitcher?

If I can talk you out of it, then I've done you and pitching a favor. If I can talk you out of it, then you really don't want to be a pitcher. It's something you have to want very much. The price is higher than you can imagine.

Pitching looks like a lot of fun — and it is. But being a pitcher is something else entirely.

You go to the ball park and you see the pitcher standing there in the middle of the diamond. He stands on a hill like a king with the grass of the infield cut away all around him. He's the center of attraction. He gets the third out and walks comfortably off the mound toward the dugout with the knowledge that he was better than the other side. Everybody else runs off the field, but the pitcher walks, lingering in the eye and the mind of the fans.

It looks like fun.

But think of what it took to get him there. If he's any good. If he's going to be better than the other side consistently and for very long, he had to be willing to give it an awful lot of his life. Maybe it's more than you're willing to give.

Think of the hottest day you've ever experienced. It's a

summer afternoon in St. Louis or New York and a hundred degrees in the shade. The stands block what little breeze there is.

You're pitching in the sixth inning of a close game, and you're beginning to feel sick to your stomach. Your uniform is so wet it feels like a weight. The sweat runs down your forehead into the corner of your eye as you try to concentrate on the batter, who's been resting in the cool of the dugout. You try to wipe the sweat from your eyes with your sleeve, but you've already rubbed your eyelids raw. The drops of sweat sting.

You take a deep breath, and the air you pull in would bake bread. You can see the heat shimmering in waves above the ground. In fact it looks like there's a cool pool of water just behind the shortstop. You'd really like to be on the beach someplace.

But there are eight other guys on the field and all those on the bench depending on you to throw the ball over the plate, to get the ball in such a position that the hitter can't hit it too hard. If you can't get the thought of the beach out of your mind, then you don't want to be a pitcher. Nobody else wants you to be a pitcher, either.

I remember being in boot camp in the Marine Corps when I was eighteen, before I was at all sure I could ever be a major league pitcher. I was being punished — I forget why — by being made to do a rifle drill. I'll never forget that.

Order arms. Right shoulder arms. Order Arms. Hold the weapon at your side, snap it up and place it on your shoulder. Snap it away, and then place it down at your side at attention. Over and over again. I must have done that for two solid hours one night. It was so tiring they had to change instructors in the middle of the drill. And they were just watching me. At the end I was dead. I didn't care how well I did the drill. Many times I just threw the rifle down.

It was all part of the psychology of being a Marine. They were going to keep only those who could stand it, and they tried hard to make guys quit. At the same time they kept pushing at

8

each individual, appealing to him, that he was different — he was a Marine: Marines are different.

The connection with pitching is that the instructors were saying, you can continue where others can't. The difference is that I want to pitch. I wasn't doing those up-and-on-shoulders because I wanted to. Pitching, I can push myself because I want to. Even when I'm tired, I can drive myself because I want to. I love being a pitcher. I love winning. I don't need somebody behind me screaming and calling me names to make me do my best.

In the service they had to drive us until we reached the point of having pride in being a Marine, as they saw it. If you're going to be a pitcher, you better have that same kind of pride the moment you step toward the mound and all the time in between when you're getting ready. Or don't be a pitcher.

I love pitching. I have the highest regard for pitchers. I think that's clear by now. But no matter how long I play, the only regret is that I didn't get to play every day. An individual playing every day has to have the most fun in baseball. He's competing every day, satisfying his desire to play the game.

In the game's higher levels a pitcher gets in the game every fourth or fifth day. There are times you sit on the bench between games, and it becomes long and drawn out. Many times I wished I had another position to play. I'd love to be in the infield someplace — someplace where there's a lot of action, where you're involved all the time. I'd even be a catcher, as grinding as that position is.

The pitcher's responsibility is to make the time between his pitching assignments something that will keep his mind occupied and stimulate him to work, to be ready. And if he's ready that one day makes up for all the lost time, all the time spent sitting on the bench waiting for his chance. That's the satisfaction.

I don't think there's any satisfaction in sports greater than what a pitcher feels. The pitcher is where it all begins. He has the ball. Nobody else can do a thing until he throws it. The best of shortstops must wait until the ball is hit to him. The best of hitters

9

come to bat maybe four or five times in a game. All twenty-seven outs belong to the pitcher. If he pitches poorly the best of teams can't save him. If he pitches well he can win with the worst of teams. Look at Steve Carlton. He won 27 games with a dreadful Philadelphia team in 1972.

Of course, this is a terrible responsibility. You have to be willing to carry it.

The sitting part, the time lost between games is mostly the situation with the professional player. Kids should experience playing more than one position. When I was young I was lucky, I played every position in Little League except first base and right field. The young player should get a taste of what it's like to be an infielder. He should try the outfield. And he should see if pitching gives him the satisfaction.

Part of the scene in the big-league ball park is the crowd of fans who want autographs before a game. Signing this many is often hard work, but these are the people who pay the rent. *(Newsday photo)*

The older you get the more you realize what's involved with being a pitcher. As you get into a higher league and then the next higher one, you find pitching takes more and more of your time. You find the number of pitchers playing other positions fewer and fewer. By the time you get to the college level, pitchers are pitchers and infielders are infielders — there aren't many players there who can do double duty.

In some respects pitching is easier than almost any other position. You don't have to run fast; you don't need the best eyesight. You don't even need great coordination. I've seen pitchers who had difficulty walking and chewing gum at the same time and pitchers with eyeglasses as thick as the bottoms of soda bottles.

You don't have to be an athlete to be a pitcher. There are pitchers in the major leagues who aren't. But it certainly helps. All the other things that go into pitching: fielding, running, running the bases, helping yourself at bat come so much easier to an athlete than to a nonathlete.

Now we're getting into areas that I feel make throwing the ball almost a secondary part of being a pitcher.

I definitely feel there are so many other things to investigate and learn before we even talk about throwing a fastball past a hitter. It's also more fun to play the game when you can consider yourself a baseball player rather than just the fellow who stands on the hill and throws the ball.

In one of the years Bob Gibson won twenty games pitching for the Cardinals, he played a part in producing a run in five of his first six wins. That's why I work in spring training trying to move the runner from first to second. I work on bunting, on my fielding. In spring training, when there isn't time for the pitchers to bat against live pitching, I go to the pitching machine to make myself as good a hitter as I can be.

It's a dreadful feeling to lose a 2-1 game because you were sloppy covering first base, or know you could have helped score the tying run if you'd been able to bunt a runner into scoring position.

11

These are all things you learn little by little all the way up — from the time you begin in Little League — including all the time you spend just running in the outfield to stay in shape. That's what makes you a pitcher.

The rewards are great. That's entirely on a personal basis. I can only tell you what it is for Tom Seaver.

Pitching is the most important part of the game — up to 80 percent of it, if the pitching is good. If you have good pitching you can win. It's generally accepted that good pitching can stop good hitting.

Pitching is the most satisfying, most rewarding, fulfilling thing I can do. I've worked so hard at it for so long that to pitch well and win is tremendous. Each time is still a great pleasure.

There are two parts to it. There's pitching well, and there's winning. You can pitch well and lose, certainly, and still get a measure of satisfaction in having done your best. But if you pitch well and win you harvest the whole crop. Nothing is spoiled.

You have to feel the challenge, too. It's more rewarding to win a 1-0 game than a 6-0 game, even though your physical part may be precisely the same. The 1-0 game is a challenge of all you have, a demand of all the concentration you can put into it. You have to make every pitch just right, or you don't win, 1-0.

I think that's what it must be like for the best of the relief pitchers, fellows like Tug McGraw or Sparky Lyle. Almost every time they're in a game they face the greatest challenge — the late innings, a close score, runners on base. Getting out of a jam and saving a game like that must be a great sensation.

I've done a minimum of relief pitching; each man tries to do what he's best suited for. I've been McGraw's teammate for several years, and I know how his and my approach to the game are similar as a relief pitcher and as a starter.

To both of us there's no satisfaction like having a job to do and doing it — if you enjoy good hard work and doing it the way it should be done.

To work hard and do your job the best you possibly can on

that specific occasion can be the most rewarding thing. I'd like to have every young man grow up and approach life with my approach to pitching. It makes no difference for personal satisfaction whether you're a pitcher, a doctor, or a carpenter. Whatever you do you have to satisfy yourself.

How many times in school do you wonder, could I have earned an A or a B instead of my C, if I had really worked at it?

The most rewarding times I've ever had pitching grew out of that. There was the fourth game of the 1969 World Series, the game in which Ron Swoboda made his great diving catch in right field. That was so great for the importance it had to the team. And there was the near-perfect game I pitched against the Cubs in July of that season. That was great to me, because it was so close to all the things I tried to learn and do from the first time I tried to pitch in Little League.

My control was pinpoint. All my pitches were very, very

Sometimes you can read the concentration in my expression. This is a curveball to the Orioles in the 1969 World Series. *(AP photo)*

13

good: fastball, curve, slider and even a couple of changeups. My
selection of pitches was good; I was setting up pitches right. Just
everything seemed to be right. There weren't many difficult plays
for the fielders. The Cubs were hitting the balls I wanted them to
hit. They were hitting balls in the air on pitches I wanted them to
hit in the air, balls on the ground that I wanted hit on the ground.

I can remember Billy Williams, an awfully good hitter who
seems to hit line drives all the time, popping out a couple of times,
and Ron Santo flying out 400 feet to straightaway center, which
was exactly what I was trying to get him to do.

Santo, who is strong, tries to pull the ball, and I was throwing
outside to him, just hard enough so he couldn't pull. Right where I
wanted to put the ball. I didn't intend for him to hit it that far,
but I did want him to hit to the deepest part of the park.

It was an incredible night for me. The first twenty-five Cubs
went out in order. I had one out in the ninth inning, and I was
pitching a perfect game. There had been only eight of them
pitched since 1900. Then Jim Qualls, a light hitter who played

center field mostly for his defense, got a single — not a very hard hit but a clean single. And I wound up with a one-hitter. That's almost as good as you can ever do.

I was aware of what was going on all the time. The stands in Shea Stadium were full, and the noise poured out of those fans. But I had to separate myself. I knew what was possible and getting more and more possible — and how remarkable it was. But I still had my job to do. But when I got off the mound, when the game was over, then I was in awe of what had happened. "My God, it really was a fascinating game, a fascinating experience."

It was like having a magic wand that night, reaching out and touching the ball to a spot I had picked in my mind. That's the reward for all the preparation, everything you've done. All of a sudden you hit the tennis ball, shoot the basket, throw the pitch, and it does exactly what you want it to do. You say, "Wow! Look at that!"

A fastball low and away can be just an absolute thing of beauty because you've worked so hard for it. You've done

The last pitch of a memorable game in 1970. It was the third strike to Al Ferrara of the Padres for my nineteenth strike-out of the game, tying a record; and ten in a row, which set a record. We won 2-1. *(AP photos, p. 14, 15)*

15

everything. If it's the third strike on the third out in the bottom of the ninth inning and you're winning, 1-0, all of those things behind you come into play, and it becomes an enormous experience.

You get so involved working toward it, you really don't think about where you are. It's the World Series and the importance and thrill of it can overwhelm you if you're not deep enough into what you're trying to do. Millions are watching on TV, there are 50,000 in the stands, and your job is so important to you it dominates everything.

The fans, The President. Nobody and nothing else count. Nothing counts except you and your job.

There are times, after a good game, when it's fun to relax and run over the highlights of the game. *(Newsday photo)*

16

2

Getting Ready

The most important part of pitching is, of course, throwing the ball. That's what everything leads up to, but in a real sense it's the last thing you think about.

Before you throw a single pitch, you have to be ready. You have to be strong and you have to be in shape, or you can't do your job. You may have a great fastball, but it isn't much use very long if you aren't in condition.

A pitcher has to work harder to keep himself in shape than a player who's playing every day. Other players play every day, and playing keeps them in shape. A pitcher is in the game every four or five days. On that one day he tears his body down. His job for the next three or four days is getting his body ready again for his next assignment.

A high school pitcher doesn't have the same kind of time schedule as a major league pitcher, but he also has to make good use of his lag time.

The basic thing is to make the most of your body. There's not much any of us can do for a small person to make him bigger, but you can make the most of your size. You may be small, but you can be strong. Underline that in your mind.

Bobby Schantz of the Athletics, who was the American League's Most Valuable Player in 1952, was no bigger than a lot of high school freshmen, but he was strong. He had trained his body to do all the necessary things. He was an outstanding pitcher, and he could run, field, and handle a bat, too.

17

YOUR BODY

You throw the ball with your arm, but you want your legs to do the most work. When your legs are tired, your arm can't do its job.

When I've worked hard, I can feel the fatigue in the big muscles of my back, in my thighs, and in my backside more than in my shoulder and my forearm. I am an overhand pitcher, and I know that if my legs get tired I have a tendency to drop my arm down closer to sidearm. I don't pitch well sidearm.

So I have no trouble getting interested in running between starts. That's where my conditioning begins.

RUNNING

Earl Weaver, who managed the Orioles to three consecutive 100-win seasons, says it's much easier to keep major league pitchers in shape than minor leaguers. He should know. He spent eleven seasons managing in the minor leagues. "In the minors, you tell the pitchers to run and they snicker and say, 'We're not going to run the ball to the plate,' " Weaver says. "They don't tell you that in the big leagues. Everybody knows how important it is."

We run wind sprints. Start at one foul line in the outfield and run to center field and walk back. If the outfield isn't available for running, mark off fifty or sixty yards for running — and wear a comfortable pair of shoes that fit well.

Always try to run with the wind. Running into the wind dries your mouth and makes you want to quit before you should.

It's a good practice to loosen up before you begin to run hard. Do a few jumping jacks to limber up (we'll talk about them a little later) or jog a little first. Don't expect to break any dash records your first lap. Work gradually into your top speed. Use the first three or four to really get loose.

If you're in a climate where you can't run outside all the time, try to find something you can do in the gym. Even running up stairs helps to build the muscles in your legs. When you do get to run outside, start light. Do eight or ten sprints for the first four days and then add two more each day until you get up to eighteen or twenty. As you keep working, those eighteen or twenty laps get easier and easier.

BETWEEN STARTS

Once you're in shape to start the season, you still have the problem of staying in shape between games you pitch. Make it as pleasant as possible. Try to run with somebody. If he sees you don't take the lazy man's way out, it will encourage him to keep working — and if you see him work, how can you cop out?

The day after you pitch have somebody throw fly balls to you. You can make a game of it, almost like going out to catch a forward pass. You run twenty yards or so, and he tosses the ball just far enough so you have to sprint another twenty to catch it. Run twelve or fourteen sprints that day after pitching, enough to work the stiffness out of your body.

On the second day extend yourself to fourteen or sixteen sprints. Run ten or twelve at a very good pace and get a good workout.

On the third day push yourself a little more. Do sixteen or eighteen — even twenty — sprints, and fourteen or fifteen of them should be done at a very good pace. Get up on your toes and dig into the sprints.

On the fourth day, the day before pitching, make it a light workout. Do eight or ten sprints and a couple at the end at your best pace.

ON YOUR OWN

It shouldn't matter to you whether the coach is watching. You know that to do your job pitching, you have to do your work in between. A pitcher doesn't do his running for his coach, a pitcher runs for himself. You have to learn that as well as

19

continually tell yourself you're not playing the game for somebody else. Know when you go out to the mound to take your turn that you're going to be completely ready.

There are times when Rube Walker, our pitching coach on the Mets, will say, "Today is a day off." Maybe it will be a day game after a night game, very hot weather, or we've had a hectic travel schedule. But if it's a day I feel I have to run, I do it anyhow.

The thing about running is to find your own style and rhythm. Find out exactly which days you should run hard. Find out what makes your body feel best. If you feel best when you work hard the day after you pitch, then do it that way.

On the day before you pitch, you should do some running, but don't wear yourself out. You should almost be ready to pitch that day. It's just a matter of putting the polish on your condition.

There have been pitchers who skimped on their work and still managed to be successful. But how good would they have been if they really gave themselves a chance? They'll never know.

Everybody in the world has a lazy spot. It's the thing you have to overcome. The guys who can overcome that are people I admire. They can go out on the days they feel least like working and do their work. Tug McGraw, an athlete as well as a fine relief pitcher, is one of those fellows who knows it pays off. When he knows he has to work, he goes out and does it. He's got himself to the point where he enjoys the running.

He feels good when he does it. When you do your running on the day after you've pitched, you're stiff, tired, and ragged. But at the end of the workout, you experience a kind of a refreshed feeling. The blood is flowing through your system, all the stiffness is out, and you feel more like a human being than you did.

A LITTLE BIT OF TORTURE

20

The most punishing exercise and one of the most useful for conditioning is one called pickups. We do it in spring training to build up legs and lungs, although it feels more like destruction.

Get a friend — or, better, somebody you hate — to work with you. Stand face to face about five feet apart. He rolls a ball about ten feet to your right; you move quickly to it, pick it up, and toss it back to him. Then he rolls it to the other side. Start by doing twenty-five of these.

That's about as hard as you can work in a contained time. It can make your stomach turn inside out. And when it doesn't, it feels as if it will. But don't forget: Do your pickups, and you can give them back to the other fellow. No laughing, please.

READY, EXERCISE

There are two basic kinds of exercises that can be useful to you. There are limbering exercises, ones you use to loosen up before going on to something else. And there are exercises to build muscular strength. I don't think either is very much fun. They are two more things you have to push yourself to accomplish because of their benefits.

Remember that baseball is a game of flexibility more than strength. Don't overdo exercises to the point that they bind you. Great arm and muscle development may be just the right thing for a defensive tackle, but it's just a handicap for a pitcher. For that reason I would confine all the building exercises, including all weight training, to the offseason.

LOOSENING UP

Stretching exercises are the best way to protect yourself from the pulled muscle that comes from running hard while your body is still cold. Stretch all of the muscles you can.

Jumping Jack — stand feet together, arms at your side. As you bring your hands together overhead, spread your legs. Then down and together again.

Situp — Sit on the ground with your legs spread, hands

behind your head. Touch your right elbow to your left knee, back down and then left elbow to right knee. After you get into good shape, try touching your forehead to your knee.

Kickup — Do it as if you were punting a football without a ball. Kick your right foot up as high as you can, then the left.

Stepover — Standing, cross your right foot over your left and touch the ground in front of your toes.

Reachover — On the ground, extend one leg in front and fold the other to the side and behind. Try to reach both hands as far over the extended foot as possible. Then reverse.

Bodybender — Stand with your feet spread about twelve inches, hands locked overhead. Lean your body firmly to the right, then up and lean to the left.

Despite the look of pain on my face, this is a good
exercise and one that all the Mets go through in
spring training: It is a variation of the Reach-
Over. With one leg folded behind me, I try to touch
my forehead to the knee of the extended leg. It's
fine for stretching winter-lazy muscles. (UPI photo)

Shoulder Roll — Standing, extend your arms to the sides and make small circles with them. Gradually increase the size of the circles. Don't do too many of these.

If you do these eight exercises briefly before a workout, you can save yourself a lot of pain and lost time.

GETTING STRONG

The best thing that happened to me was a strenuous summer job in which I had to lift heavy crates that brought raisins in from the fields. A machine emptied the raisins, but somebody had to get the empty boxes off and they were heavy. They were called "sweat boxes," which was exactly right. I was actually smaller than almost everybody in high school, but that job and the six months I spent in the Marine Corps built up my whole body. A Columbia University football coach used to try to get his players summer jobs pedaling Good Humor bicycles to build up their legs. That works.

I don't believe in trying to lift big, heavy weights. There's nothing wrong with being strong, but you've got to be able to move and be free. I like weights in a controlled manner. Take light weights, and do them often. Do isometrics: Pushing your left hand against your right; try to lift the chair your sitting on. Do them in the offseason.

Here's a set of exercises I do with a twelve-pound dumbell. You can begin with a five-pound weight or with a fat textbook.

These exercises build up your upper arm, shoulder, and chest. For balanced development do the same exercise with left arm and right.

Holding the weight over your right shoulder, lift it straight up and let it down. Do it five times, then do it with the other arm.

Hold the weight over your right shoulder and let it back down behind the shoulder. Do it five times, then do it with the other arm.

23

Hold the weight straight down at your thigh, palm toward your leg. Lift it straight out to the side as high as your shoulder, then let it down slowly. Do it five times, then repeat with the other arm.

Hold the weight at your side with the back of your hand facing forward. Raise it to the front to shoulder height with palm down, then let it down slowly. Do it five times, then repeat on the other side.

Hold the weight at your side the same way and raise it to the rear as high as you can without hurting yourself.

Find time to do the whole cycle three times a day, two or three times a week. As you go along you can increase the repetitions of each exercise to seven in a cycle and then to ten.

Get an old baseball bat and a three-foot length of rope. Nail the rope to the bat and tie a five-pound weight to the other end. Hold the bat in front at arm's length; raise the weight by rotating

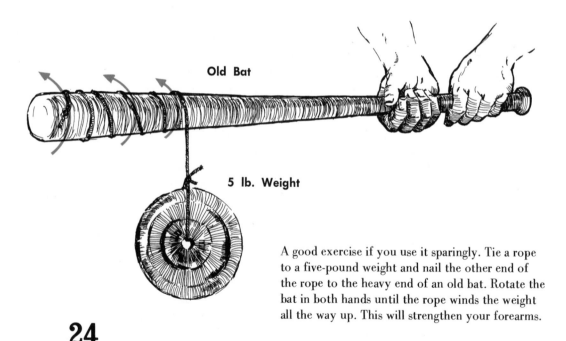

Old Bat

5 lb. Weight

A good exercise if you use it sparingly. Tie a rope to a five-pound weight and nail the other end of the rope to the heavy end of an old bat. Rotate the bat in both hands until the rope winds the weight all the way up. This will strengthen your forearms.

it with both hands. That's a good forearm exercise for hitters, especially. Pitchers should do it only occasionally.

Also keep a sponge ball handy. Squeeze it in your hand until the muscles begin to tire.

YOU ARE WHAT YOU EAT

Diet is one of the important factors few people think about. You want to eat foods that will let you pitch a full ballgame. It's not just a one-day thing on the day you pitch. Eat well-balanced meals every day. It helps you keep healthy and to build up your body. It also helps make your muscles bounce back quickly.

Your school dietician or health instructor can help you lay out a well-balanced diet.

Don't have a heavy meal before a workout. I prefer to eat four or five hours before I pitch or have a heavy workout. If you're going to school you'd obviously have to miss either lunch or the game if you stuck to that schedule. But you certainly shouldn't eat for at least an hour before practice. Don't drink milk before a workout; it makes it difficult to keep your mouth fresh.

When you're pitching you sweat out fluids from your body. You have to replace them, especially on a hot day. Of course, you can't replace all the fluids you lose while you're pitching. Don't drown yourself with water, but a little cool water — not to cold — between innings is fine. The energy-refresher drinks are good too; they leave a pleasant taste in your mouth. When your mouth tastes dry if magnifies the tired feeling in your body. Some players feel that chewing gum helps them stay refreshed while relaxing them.

I drink some soda between innings, but just a couple of swallows. Of course, if you drink a couple of swallows after an inning and go out to pitch again, when you get back there won't be anything left in the bottle. You have to find a good hiding place.

Salt tablets are useful to prevent muscle cramps in hot weather. I take two before a game. Some trainers give them during a game.

25

SMOKING — DON'T

Enough has been written about it. You ought to understand by now. Obviously, it can't help you. Your lungs need all the oxygen they can get.

SLEEP

Mothers, fathers, teachers, and coaches have been telling you to get enough sleep as long as you can remember. I'll tell you one more time. You can't get enough rest just the night before you pitch. You have to do it night after night.

When you're tired you just think about being tired, and it cuts your concentration as well as what your body can do. When we play a night game in St. Louis and go to Chicago for a day game the next day, about the seventh inning all I want is to find a place to lie down. When you haven't had enough rest before a practice, you get a lousy workout. Without sufficient rest you get into lazy, fatigued habits, and the practice does you more harm than good.

You have to realize that you have to be your own coach. If you try to fool the coach into thinking you've been getting enough rest and run out of gas on the mound, who have you really fooled?

There are lots of ways to fool coaches and managers. Players have been doing that for years and years in the big leagues. There's one favorite story about a player who moved so quickly at night that he couldn't do much running around during the game. The manager was determined to put a stop to the practice.

He waited in the lobby of the hotel shortly before the curfew, and waited, and waited, and waited. At 3 AM he still hadn't seen his man. He decided to check the man's room, and leave word with the roommate that the manager wanted to see the player the next day at the ball park.

The manager knocked on the player's door, and who should answer but the very same man under study, pajamaed and smiling.

"I've been sitting in the lobby all night. I never saw you come in," the manager said. "How did you do it?"

"I'll tell you, if you promise not to fine me," the player said.

The manager felt he had to know—just out of curiosity—so he agreed.

"Remember the laundry cart that was wheeled through the lobby about twenty minutes ago? Well, I gave the laundry attendant five bucks to cover me with sheets and get me to the elevator."

The point is if you fool the coach, so what?

There are times, too, when you'll be in bed, but there will be no sleep. When I'm too nervous to sleep, I get up and read until I fall asleep. The night before I pitched my first Little League game, I don't think I slept at all.

You just lie there and think of what it's going to be like. If you can't sleep the night before the championship game, you're not alone. Everyone else is wide awake, too.

THE BALL

Now you're ready to pick up the ball. It's round, white, and hard. You haven't seen it since last season. Take it easy, especially if the weather is cold. It's a long season.

Throw five minutes the first day and no breaking balls. Skip a day, and throw five minutes on the third. Throwing every other day, gradually work up to seven, ten, twelve minutes. During the first intrasquad or practice game, you shouldn't throw more than fifty or sixty pitches.

You can't go hard the first days. Play a nice firm game of catch. Certainly not as hard as you can. That's a good way to tear muscles.

27

3

Clothing and Equipment

Let's think of the body you were blessed with and the equipment from the team or sporting goods store as a single unit. You have to select the equipment according to the body, and you have to take care of both. You can't run if your feet are blistered by ill-fitting shoes. You can't field well if your glove isn't right for your hand.

Since you can't do a whole lot to change your body, you have to chose your equipment wisely.

YOUR GLOVE

The first piece of equipment you become involved with becomes your best friend. Love your glove. A good one makes it much more fun to play the game. One that isn't right for you spoils a lot of things. A professional model costs a lot of money and probably isn't suitable for anybody younger than a high school senior, anyhow.

Pick one that feels right on your hand when you move it about. Don't pick one that's too heavy to control or makes your arm and hand tired from sheer weight. It's also foolish to buy an overly large glove with the idea of growing into it. It's better to buy a less expensive glove that fits.

Basically, a pitcher uses a glove that's bigger than an infielder's glove and smaller than an outfielder's. A pitcher needs a glove large enough to hide the ball but small enough to be moved quickly after a batted ball. Never mind the autograph on it. Pick the one that suits you, not the one with your favorite player's name.

The first glove I remember was a Harvey Kuenn model. I was trying to get the last out of a perfect game in Little League, and the eighteenth and last batter struck out. I threw the glove into the air and hid my eyes in my hands. The Harvey Kuenn model was very good for throwing into the air.

Remember, the glove does its job when it enables you to catch the ball better and protects your hand, but don't expect the glove to take all the sting out of a hard throw. That's up to the way you learn to give with the impact; it's called soft hands. A stiff, heavily padded glove will cut the sting, but you won't be able to catch well with it.

In the spring almost everything will sting a little, but your hands toughen up quickly, and you soon get the sense of giving with the ball.

You will need a glove with firm body, enough to hold it's shape when you catch a line drive. Try to keep it firm. Don't throw it around. Find a place to put your glove when you're not wearing it, and keep it there. That precaution will keep your glove from being stepped on, and you'll be able to find it when you want it.

CARE AND BREAKING IN

I like to take a new glove, moisten the pocket area with water and place two balls in the pocket. Then I wrap some string around it to hold the balls in place. That helps form the pocket. I prefer to have a glove that folds the long way, across the heel of the glove, and that's the way I keep it tied for a few days.

Then you catch with the glove. Use one that's already broken in when you're pitching, and break in a new one when you're warming up or shagging flies in the outfield.

I don't use oil on my glove unless it's absolutely necessary. Oil

29

tends to make the glove heavy and takes away a lot of the firmness. Use oil only if the glove becomes too stiff, or if the leather begins to crack—inside or out. Make sure the lacing isn't dried out. If it gets worn thin, a shoemaker can replace it with fresh leather thongs.

If your glove gets wet in a rainstorm or caught under a sprinkler, rub it as dry as you can, and then leave it out in the air to dry. Don't put it on a heater or radiator. That will ruin the leather.

In the winter put a ball in the pocket of your glove and wrap it up in an old dishtowel, then put it in a cool place away from heat.

SHOES

They have to fit. Absolutely. When you try them on, make sure you're wearing the same kind of socks you'll wear on the field. If the shoes are too loose, they'll slip and give you blisters, If they're too small, they'll cramp your feet.

If you're buying expensive shoes, consider that the best light leather stretches on your feet, and many professional players buy a size or half size smaller than street shoes to account for the stretch.

Buy a toeplate, too. It's an aluminum piece that attaches to the toe of your shoe—right shoe for right-handed throwers—and is tied in with the laces. That protects the leather of the shoe when you push off the rubber and it's a lot less costly to replace a worn toeplate than a whole pair of shoes.

Also keep your shoes polished. This protects them from dirt and moisture. You ought to take pride in the way you look as well as in the way you play.

After you've worn baseball shoes and they're damp with sweat or rain, stuff them with paper, or use shoe trees, and let them dry naturally away from a heater.

30

If your feet are sore at the start of the season, there's nothing at all wrong with doing your running in a comfortable pair of basketball or tennis shoes. They're used for that purpose by enough big leaguers. Don't think it's sissy stuff; just get in your running.

FROM THE INSIDE OUT

Your clothes serve two functions. They keep you warm, and they protect you.

Lets start with your socks. They have to be clean. You can wear the thin sanitary socks that go up to your knee under the standard uniform socks. I wear two pair of sanitary socks for a little better cushion and greater sweat absorption. Some players wear a pair of sanitaries and a pair of sweat socks. Find out what's comfortable for you, as long as they're clean. *I'll repeat: As long as they're clean.* Athlete's foot or an infected blister doesn't help your pitching.

Wear a T-shirt. That's the most comfortable thing to have next to your skin when you're doing the kind of work pitching is. Have an extra one around to change into on a hot day.

I have a woolen sweatshirt, a long-sleeved cotton one, and a cotton one with short sleeves, depending on the weather. Even on the hottest days it's a good idea to wear sleeves that go down to your elbow. On cold days you can wear a turtleneck to protect your neck and shoulders, if it's comfortable.

Don't fool yourself about the heat. It may seem like an inferno when you're on the mound or even sitting in the stands, but you don't want your muscles to cool off and tighten between innings or when a breeze comes up. You try to keep the body heat in on most days.

So in the middle of the summer, especially at night, a pair of long johns are useful. They can be light cotton, but they should extend down below your knees. Remember, you're trying to make

31

your thigh muscles carry a lot of the load, and you don't want them to stiffen.

On days when I'm not worried about the cold, I wear a pair of midthigh cotton briefs. Some players prefer to wear a supporter under the cotton shorts. Others feel more comfortable with the shorts under the supporter, thinking it protects their skin from rubbing and irritation.

But *wear them both*. Also wear the kind of supporter that provides for an aluminum or plastic protective cup. You can take the cup out when you do your running, but wear it when you're pitching or taking fielding practice. Don't forget it. A ground ball can take funny bounces, a line drive can deflect off your glove. Pitchers have been hurt because they didn't wear a cup. You may find it uncomfortable to wear at the beginning, but you'll get used to it—and you have to do it.

Have a jacket handy. A light windbreaker can keep your

My locker. If you look closely you will see clothes that fit the weather. There's a windbreaker at the left, short- and long-sleeve cotton shirts, long-sleeve woolen shirts, and several pairs of shoes. The gloves are on the top shelf so they don't get stepped on. *(Joe De Maria photo)*

muscles from chilling when you're on the bases or in the dugout between innings. On a colder day have something heavier. You don't gain anything by pretending you're braver than the cold.

Don't try to fit yourself into a uniform that's too tight because you think it looks flashy. Yet when you're pitching the most important thing is to have freedom of movement without having a lot of fabric flapping around your arms and legs.

Keep your uniform socks up with rubber bands, garters or adhesive tape. You don't want them so tight that you cut off the flow of blood, but a pair of socks that fall down when you run to field a bunt is very distracting as well as being unstylish.

I showed up at my first Little League game with my socks on backwards. The high part of the stirrup goes to the back and the low-cut part to the front.

Tuck your shirt in. Keep your cap in good condition. The rules say that you have to wear it, so get used to it. Part of playing well is how you feel in your uniform. Have pride in both.

KEEP IT CLEAN

You must have read about keeping clean someplace before, right? It's worth repeating. Don't linger in the shade after a game in a wet uniform. Take a shower to cool down your body. If you can't get to a shower—if you have to take a bus home—put on a dry shirt and a jacket.

A shower doesn't have to take a long time to do the job. In fact, it can take hardly any time at all as I learned from an infielder named Wilbur Huckle, when we were at Jacksonville together. He holds the minor league record for going from uniform to streetclothes in the least possible time.

If he were a better third baseman, he'd probably be close to the major league record, too.

Almost every day Huckle would win a fast-dressing contest without ever knowing he was in a race. He would be playing third

33

base in the ninth inning and begin to unbutton his shirt with two out, as he always did. On the end of the bench in the dugout there would be a teammate with his shirt open all the way down and his shoes untied, waiting for the last out. He'd almost be in a sprinter's crouch.

As soon as the last out was made, the teammate would break for the clubhouse, pull off his uniform, and dive under the shower. Rubbing the water off his body as quickly as he could, he'd look around, and there would go Wilbur. His shower was done, he was dressed, and he was on his way out the door.

Once when Huckle was in the low minors his team was in an awful losing streak, as happened often in the Met organization in those years. The way I heard the story, they lost still another game, and their manager could hardly wait for them to get into the clubhouse before he began hollering. "Sit down," he insisted. "This has gone too damn far. Sit down and think about your mistakes. Nobody's taking a shower until I say so."

The manager stormed at his players and behind him, there was Huckle, toweling himself dry. He'd already had his shower. He'd been in there even before the manager issued his stormwarning.

Make sure your supporter is clean. Wash it after each wearing. Jock itch can be an awful pain. There are ointments that cure it, but they burn like anything.

Athlete's foot can keep you out of the lineup, too. Make sure your feet are dry after a shower. There are powders and sprays to prevent athlete's foot, too. It's much easier to prevent athlete's foot than to cure it.

Make sure your towel is laundered frequently. You can get some very unpleasant skin infections from using a dirty towel. And only use your own.

Have a pair of shower shoes to wear. They don't cost much, but they can be worth a lot. Get a splinter from an old locker room floor, and you'll know what I mean. Buy a pair you can slip on over your socks, so you can remove your spikes on the bus or carry them in and out of the dressing room.

UNTIL THE DOCTOR COMES

If you have an injury don't try to hide it from the coach. He can get help for you that will heal a pulled muscle or a strain better than anything you can do for yourself. You have to be able to help the coach understand the nature of your injury. You don't want to baby yourself, but you don't want a small injury to grow to something larger than could have been treated early. You don't want to spoil a whole season, because you pretended the ache in your shoulder was nothing.

Lots of little things, though, you'll have to take care of yourself. You get little nicks and scrapes all the time. Keep the area clean and use an antiseptic.

If you feel a blister forming on your foot, don't try to open it yourself. Put a bandage on it to protect against further irritation. If it's small and opens, use antiseptic and a bandage. If it's extensive tell the coach.

There will be days, too, especially when you are getting into condition, when you'll ache all over. Take a quick shower after practice, and then when you get home leisurely sit and soak in the warmest bath you can tolerate. That good hot water can do wonders for the circulation in sore muscles.

Remember, your body is the most important piece of equipment you'll ever have—and the one you can't replace in a sporting goods store.

Once you've got your body in shape and your uniform on, we can talk about playing the game and learning to pitch.

4

Attitude and Approach

There are things you never forget as long as you play ball. One of them is a thing called love.

It's a big word that includes a lot of things that are nothing like other meanings of the word. It's the kind of feeling that's there when the last out of the championship game is made, and you hug your teammate out of the sheer joy of it with the understanding that you and your teammates have worked so hard toward a common goal.

And it's there in the deepest disappointments. It was in the clubhouse for Willie Stargell, when the Pirates lost the final game of the National League playoff in 1972. Stargell had been a great player all season and had a dismal playoff. He had one hit in fifteen at-bats. One more at the right time could have sent the Pirates instead of the Reds, to the World Series. Stargell knew it, and he felt it.

"He's the type of person who feels those things," said pitcher Steve Blass, who sort of understood what was going on in Stargell's mind. "I hope he realizes he's no lesser man in the eyes of the fellows who play with him," Blass said. "It's been fun playing with him. He's not a Superman. He's just a super man."

That was love in its purest form. It was there on the Mets at its sweetest, when we won the World Series in 1969. The feeling of what you've accomplished and the pride you have in yourself and your uniform is shared exactly by the men wearing the same uniform.

When you get an entire team that prepares itself fully and does all the things it can, you get a very close feeling of teamwork. You know all the little things that came about because you made them come about as a team. Things happened for you because players were willing to put their minds to a situation and predetermine what they'd do on every possible play instead of waiting for things to happen.

That's the best possible feeling of being an athlete.

Often you see people who haven't worked as hard as they might have. You see them in spring training all the time. There's the infielder who doesn't take his full ration of ground balls, the pitcher who doesn't do his running or take his pickups. How about the former high school player who doesn't do his job. Is he going to look back on that one championship game he lost by one run and wonder if he could have won and gone further, if he hadn't skipped his running twice in that last week?

You often see players who aren't moved by winning or losing. They feel all right if they've done well themselves. But those are rarely the best players.

There's something else to that, too. I know I don't feel as depressed by losing as I did when I first came up to the big leagues. I've learned that losing has to be part of the game. Hardly any pitcher wins more often than twice for every game he loses: That's a 20-10 record. Almost no team escapes without losing once for every two it wins.

You have to learn the reality of losing. There are just some days when you get beat.

When you've done everything you can but still lose, those are the days that hurt the least. You can't ask anything more of yourself.

After he competes on the field, the athlete's feeling should be, "I've given one hundred percent. I've done my absolute best at playing baseball today." That's what you owe yourself as a baseball player—that you've adequately prepared yourself mentally and physically. It's no excuse saying that it was somebody else's fault that you lost. Your error or somebody else's

37

will be a part of the game forever, because baseball is, after all, a game played by human beings.

You just have to think, "I've done my best and have nothing to regret." That's how you live with yourself as a ballplayer.

Once in the International League, in my first year as a professional, when warming up before an important game, I was just overcome by my own nervousness. I was standing there at attention for the National Anthem, and about "What so proudly we hailed . . ." I threw up. I never took my hat away from my heart.

You can't live like that and pitch in thirty or forty games a season. You'd be a mental wreck.

But you do get a flutter of nerves no matter how much experience or confidence you have.

In my first All-Star Game, in Anaheim in 1967, I was in the bullpen not expecting to pitch. Then the game went into the fifteenth inning and the phone rang. Jeff Torborg told me I had to warm up. The National League took a 2-1 lead, and all of a sudden I'm being called upon to pitch.

I was just in awe of everything that was going on. I had dressed next to Henry Aaron and Willie Mays, all the players who were my idols when I was a youngster. The whole experience was too much for me to assimilate.

But when I went onto that mound with a 2-1 lead, I wasn't the little kid any more. I wasn't playing for North Fresno Rotary in the Little League or for Dodge Laundry in the Babe Ruth League. I was Tom Seaver, big-league pitcher, and I knew what I had to do. I had trained myself as a professional athlete. I knew how to pitch, and I had confidence I could get them out.

I got the first two batters out, and Carl Yastrzemski was coming up. It was against all the rules of baseball strategy to put the tying run on base, but Yaz was a left-handed power hitter, and I didn't want him to tie the score. I pitched very carefully and walked him. The next hitter was right-handed Ken Berry, and I struck him out on four pitches. I did know what I was doing.

I had confidence under all my nervousness—and confidence is such a vital thing. It's hard to have confidence before you've really accomplished something, but sometimes you have to sell yourself a bill of goods. If you go out to the mound with negative feelings about yourself, it's certainly going to be almost impossible for you to do your best. At least you should feel you've prepared completely.

My first month or so with the Mets in the big leagues was almost a dream, except when I was pitching. When I was off the field I wondered if I belonged. That first game I pitched, the second day of the season, was against Pittsburgh with all its tough hitters. The first hitter was Matty Alou. I know you're supposed to remember everything, but I don't remember what I did with Alou except I got him out. I remember that we won, 3-2, and Chuck Estrada was the winning pitcher in relief. I was proud; I showed I was a good-enough pitcher. I could do my job.

Part of that confidence is willingness to think about yourself. Part of being a winner is knowing why you won, what you did right to make you a winner. It's also knowing what made the other team a loser. And when you lose, you should learn what made you lose and try to gain from that understanding.

One of the things you learn is adaptability. You can get some of that from playing other sports. I learned a lot of general rules about playing baseball from playing basketball in high school. I made all-city in Fresno as a senior even though I wasn't as tall as a lot of other players. I wasn't much of a shooter, either, but I could drive and play defense. Rather, I was willing to work at defense. Those skills are like control and clear thinking for a pitcher.

There are days when you can't throw a basketball in the ocean, but you can play a solid game with the other things you can do on the court.

There are days when I don't have my best stuff on the mound, but I can pitch well with my control, my physical condition, and by being as smart a pitcher as I can be. Those tools never desert you, if you've worked for them.

39

KNOW YOURSELF

You also have to learn your own limitations. Harvey Haddix, the first pitching coach I had on the Mets, made the point to me that knowing myself would be one of the most difficult things to learn. I had to know when it was foolish to think I could overpower a hitter with my fastball just because I was throwing hard. Good big-league hitters hit the best fastballs when they aren't set up properly or when they aren't thrown to the good spots. And quarterbacks have to learn even they can't complete passes to covered receivers without risk.

After a great season for the Mets in 1969 and for myself with a 25-7 record, I expected to pitch well again and the team to win again. I think we would have won again in 1970, but I pitched poorly. And I think I would have pitched better if I didn't feel it was so vital that I pitch better.

I was really pitching well early in the year, and I tried to pitch with three days' rest instead of my usual four twice in a row. I lost two and I began pressing. I was trying too hard for a while, not realizing that I had become a thrower again instead of a pitcher. I was trying so hard that I lost my composure.

I lost everything, but I think I also learned a great lesson that should be valuable for the rest of my career: I'm a human being. You have to realize your physical limits, and you have to control your emotions under almost any circumstance.

Other things began to interfere with the way I physically went about pitching my game. I just didn't function at all. The whole thing was like a gray fog, and nothing I did was right.

Then I got to tampering with the way I was pitching, and that was a mistake. You just have to relax and rely on your own natural and learned abilities. It's a hard thing to do, but you just have to relax. Having people rely on you makes pitching much more than a personal thing. If the rest of the team was winning, then my not winning wouldn't have been so burdensome.

Some of that gets back to a story I heard about the track

40

coach who had some Olympic-class sprinters and told them to run a hundred yards as hard as they could. He timed them. Then he asked them to run the same distance at three-quarters speed. The times he got at the relaxed pace were faster than those at full-out.

MISTAKES OF OTHERS

You also learn fairly quickly that you can't demand anything more from your teammates than their best. They're going to make mistakes behind you, mistakes that cost you dearly. They're also going to catch some of your mistakes. You have to live with both.

Errors are going to happen. You have to realize that the man who makes the error has to feel worse about it than you do. The greatest help you can be to a teammate—if you know he's giving you 100 percent, even if he costs you a game—is to pat him on the fanny and say, "Hang in there." That gesture doesn't say much more than that you still accept him. It's what Steve Blass was saying to Willie Stargell.

During my first year, while in Chicago, we were leading the Cubs, 1-0, in the bottom of the ninth. Working on my first shutout in the big leagues, I was doing it against a good hitting team. Don Kessinger got on base to lead off the Cubs' last chance at bat and was sacrificed to second. I struck out Billy Williams, an accomplishment in itself, and got Ron Santo to ground meekly to Bud Harrelson at shortstop. It would have been the third out, the end of the game.

Except the ball bounced under Buddy's glove, between his feet, into left field and the tying run scored. There went my first shutout in the big leagues.

I led off the top of the tenth inning with a single and was bunted to second. I went to third on a ground ball—the second out—and Al Luplow drove me home with a single through the middle. We had a 2-1 lead. I got them out one-two-three in the bottom of the ninth and won, 2-1. It was a happy moment.

41

But up the stairs in the cramped visiting clubhouse in beautiful Wrigley Field, Buddy was sitting in front of his locker with his head in his hands. He felt his entire world had just come down on top of him.

We had played together all the year before at Jacksonville in the International League. He had made so many plays for me in the big leagues—and he's over there brooding because he made an error that cost me a shutout. I went over and tried to cheer him up.

I told him, "You're going to make a lot more plays for me than you're going to boot." And all he could say was, "I lost the shutout for you."

I asked him, "How did we make out?"

He said, "We won, 2-1." He smiled. I finally got a smile out of him. He has been a great shortstop for all the years after that. We've roomed together for years after that. There was no reason for an error to make us enemies.

For years when Gary Gentry and I were teammates on the Mets, he used to suffer from things like that. It hurt him, and it hurt the others on the team. He hadn't been able to discipline himself on the mound for the times things occur—from other players or umpires. He couldn't bring himself to keep pitching his Number One thought on the mound. You have to be able to reach the point of self-discipline that nothing takes away from your Number One job.

At the instant of a lost double play, naturally your reaction is, "Damn!" But it's going to happen. Then the play is over, gone, and you have to get back to being a pitcher again. You need to be a pitcher even more then. Don't brood over what's gone by.

Bob Aspromonte, who played eleven seasons in the big leagues, told me that when he was young he was his own worst enemy. A pitcher would get him out on a pitch he thought he should have hit, and the next time he wouldn't try to just get a hit: He'd try to kill it. He'd try to hit the ball through the pitcher: I'll show you. One bad at-bat would spoil a whole day, and one bad day would spoil a whole week for him. He had to learn to outgrow that kind of thinking.

Unfortunately a pitcher doesn't get the chance to put a bad game out of his mind until his next turn. He has to wait three or four days with that bad taste in his mouth.

Mel Stottlemyre, who knows about being a twenty-game winner, says the games he loses linger the longest. He keeps thinking about what made him lose until his next start, and the time seems so much longer. When he wins, he immediately begins thinking about the next game and how he's going to put the things that made him win to work again. Then, almost before he knows it, it's his turn again.

BE PART OF THE TEAM

It's your job to learn how to put the time between starts to good use. You get your workout, as we've discussed, but you're on the bench, too, while the others are playing. You should be watching the opposing hitters—which balls they handle, which balls they hit in the air, and which they hit on the ground. On most big-league teams the next day's pitcher keeps a chart of how his team pitched against the opposing hitters.

On the bench you holler for your teammates, and maybe you can help your pitcher. If you pitched against the same team before, you can give him tips. Maybe you can spot a flaw in what he's doing.

Keep your head in the game. Just because you're not in the lineup, it doesn't mean you can't be in the ballgame.

5

Helping Yourself

One of the strongest memories I have from my rookie season comes from a defeat, but it goes a long way toward proving a point. I was a baseball player that day, not merely a pitcher.

It was the first time I pitched to Bad Henry Aaron of the Braves, my childhood hero and a person I still admire greatly as a man and as a baseball player. He hit a two-run homer that day, Denis Menke homered, and Joe Torre hit a home run in the bottom of the ninth inning to beat me, 4-3.

But I got three hits—two doubles and a single—knocked in two runs, scored one, stole a base, and pitched nine innings. I pitched fairly well—surely I didn't pitch a shutout, which is what you're always trying to do. But on that particular day I did the best I possibly could as a pitcher and helped myself as a baseball player.

Why should the other team be permitted to use nine players while you restrict your team to eight because all *you* can do is throw the ball? Reverse the idea: Why shouldn't you be able to take advantage of the other team if their pitcher can't handle the rest of the game? Help yourself.

I have a simple equation that to me summarizes so much of that idea. Hard work, dedication, concentration, plus God-given ability make you a good ballplayer. I don't forget about natural ability, but the first three maximize it. If you can't employ the first three factors, it's so easy to wipe away your talent.

THE FIELD

You should know the field you're playing on and the rules that govern the game. The baselines are ninety feet long. The distance from the pitching rubber to home plate is sixty feet, six inches. (A long time ago when the dimensions were marked on a diagram, an engineer intended to indicate sixty feet, zero inches, but his zero came out looking like a six so that's the way it's always been.)

The plate is seventeen inches wide. The hitter claims the middle part of it as all his own; you want a few inches on the edges.

Different playing fields have different distances to the outfield fences and to the fences outside of first and third bases and behind the plate. Those are all things you should know as a player at any position.

Be aware of the weather conditions and know how they affect your field. Which way is the wind blowing and how hard? Know if the field is wet and whether the footing around the mound is firm or slippery.

To field your position you're going to have to move and get over and cover first base. You're going to have to turn quickly. Know whether the dirt around first base is loose or firm. Say there's a runner on second base, two out, and you have to cover first base. Say the batter is called safe at first and the runner from second goes around third. You have to be ready to stop, turn, and throw. You have to know how quickly you can stop without falling on your rear end.

If the field is firm and your spikes catch, you can go as hard as you can. Suppose you field a bunt on a field that's wet. You turn to throw to second base for a force and fall. Then you don't get the out at second, and you don't even get the batter at first.

If the field is wet the batter may bunt for a hit. Don't be caught napping. Make sure you have your footing before you throw. You have to concede the runner a step or two advantage. If the man on first is like Lou Brock, Matty Alou, or Ralph Garr,

45

that's all they need. There's no way you're going to force somebody like that on a well-placed bunt.

As you get more experienced you'll want to know how hard the field is and how high the grass is. It may have a bearing on the way you pitch. If the grass is long you keep the ball down more to force more grounders. If the infield is as hard as it is in Pittsburgh or St. Louis, you may want to pitch higher and try to make them pop up more.

There may be just one hitter in the lineup who may benefit from a particularly hard infield. Say a Matty Alou. On a hard surface he can beat the ball into the ground and make it bounce a hundred feet in the air. By the time it comes down he's across first base. You'd have to try to make him hit it in the air.

If the wind is hard in the batter's face, you want to make him hit the ball in the air. If the wind is behind him you have to think that any ball hit in the air might be out of the park.

FIELDING YOUR POSITION

As soon as the pitcher releases the ball he becomes an infielder. Learn it at an early age. You can teach yourself to be a good fielder even if you don't have the greatest hands or reactions.

Get another pitcher or just a friend and five or six baseballs. Go through your pitching motion; as you get to the end of your delivery, have him hit the ball back to you or even throw it back to you. Grounders, line drives, and bunts.

Play pepper. Kids don't do enough of that. Every facet of the game is covered in pepper. It's a good warmup, too. Try to play some every day.

You can make it fun, too. My older brother and I used to play pepper with my dad in the backyard almost every night. He'd come home from work, we'd mow the grass, and we'd play pepper, working on fielding, hand control, and throwing control. You have to throw strikes in pepper.

46

We'd play for hours. A fielder would toss the ball maybe thirty feet to the batter, and he'd rap it back to us. Five or six of us would line up in front of the batter; if you made an error you'd go to the end of the line. If the fielders caught twenty in a row, the one at the head of the line became the batter, the batter going to the end of the line.

I learned to come around and squarely face the batter with my glove in front of my body. That's my style. Bob Gibson doesn't follow through like that. He's twisted around to the side of the mound by the force of his motion, but he's an outstanding fielder because he's such a good athlete and reacts so quickly.

If a pitcher has the coordination of a Bob Gibson, he doesn't have to change his follow through. But with slower reactions he has to change to protect himself.

There are two vital things to remember: Your gloved hand should never go behind your body during your pitching motion. And keep your eye on the ball after you deliver it.

The follow-through. Note the position of my glove: in front of the body for the quickest reaction to a batted ball. The whole body is squared around toward the plate. *(Newsday photo)*

Your glove should always be even with the front half of your body so you can be in position to protect yourself and knock down a line drive. If the glove is back of you it's going to take a lot longer to get it around to field a ball. Keep the fingers up and the open part facing the batter.

Watch where you're throwing and where the ball is going. A lot of young pitchers are so intent on their follow-through that their head is down. That's where they can get into trouble. If you don't know where the ball is you can't field your position. Even if Gibson's body is turned his eye is on the ball.

My first reaction on the mound is to protect myself. Some balls I've missed I should have fielded, but I may have lost sight of it for a moment and thought it was hit harder than it actually was. I got out of the way when I could have made a play.

POP FLIES

Let the infielders catch the pop flies. They probably have better hands than you anyway. Unless they're little, low pop flies that nobody can get to, stay out of the way. If you and your team follow that practice, there will rarely be a mixup in the infield causing a costly error.

FIELDING THE BUNT

Consider the bunted ball and the slow roller as the same play for a pitcher, except that with the bunt you have a little warning.

Remember which men in the opposing lineup can run and who can bunt for a base hit. Watch the other team take batting practice and see what they're working on.

For a right-hander, step your right foot across the line the ball is traveling and get in front of it. Field the ball with both hands even if it's stopped dead. Scoop the ball and get it into

Fielding the bunt. Step across the path of the ball with your right foot, get both hands down to field the ball, and make the throw with no loss of motion. *(Joe De Maria photo)*

throwing position in one motion. Your right foot should be planted firmly. Push off and make an overhand throw to first base. Concentrate on making a good throw. If you throw it into right field, that's two bases instead of one.

If the ball is close to the first-base line, and you can't get in front of it, get your glove in front of it, standing with your feet parallel to the line. Turn and throw just on the infield side of first base so that the fielder isn't pulled into the line of the runner.

A left-handed pitcher tries to get in front of the ball on the third-base side, pivoting for his throw to first or second by turning his back toward the plate. On a ball on the first-base side, he plants his left foot and again turns to his right to throw.

49

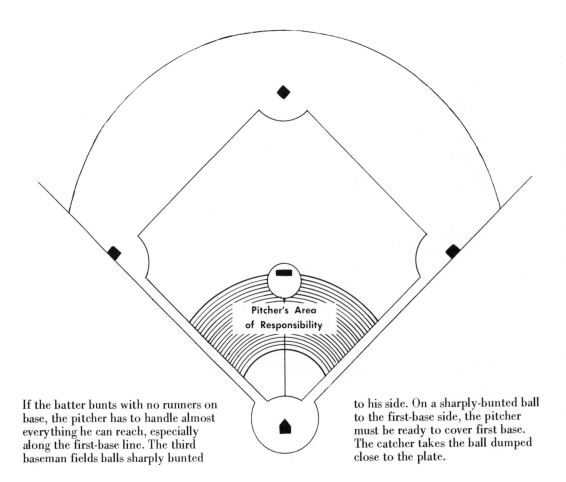

Pitcher's Area
of Responsibility

If the batter bunts with no runners on base, the pitcher has to handle almost everything he can reach, especially along the first-base line. The third baseman fields balls sharply bunted to his side. On a sharply-bunted ball to the first-base side, the pitcher must be ready to cover first base. The catcher takes the ball dumped close to the plate.

If it's a sacrifice bunt, the catcher is in charge. He should yell where to make the throw. Remember, no matter how much you want the out at second, it takes a bad bunt to force a good runner. Know who's running.

When there's a runner on first, the pitcher must not make his pitch without knowing who's covering second base, where the fielders are moving. If you're throwing to second turn toward your gloved side; make the throw just to the side of the bag of the man who's covering. Try to throw chest high.

50

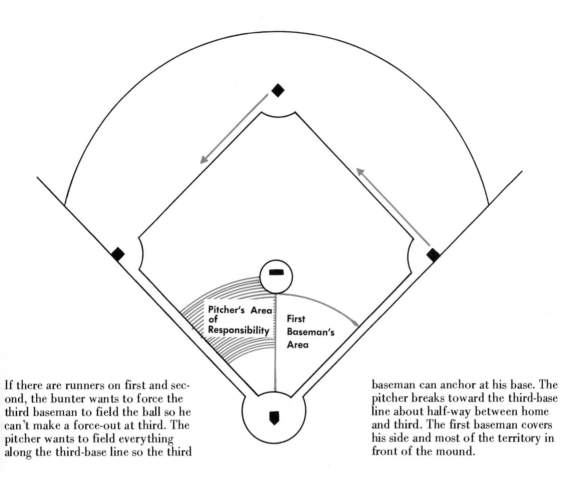

Pitcher's Area
of
Responsibility

First
Baseman's
Area

If there are runners on first and second, the bunter wants to force the third baseman to field the ball so he can't make a force-out at third. The pitcher wants to field everything along the third-base line so the third baseman can anchor at his base. The pitcher breaks toward the third-base line about half-way between home and third. The first baseman covers his side and most of the territory in front of the mound.

FIGURE THE SITUATION IN ADVANCE

If there are runners on first and second and none out, expect the ball to be bunted toward third base. The bunter wants to make the third baseman field the ball in front of the bag to eliminate the chance of a force. The pitcher should be trying to get the ball so he can get the force.

As soon as you deliver the ball, instead of breaking toward the plate as you normally would on a sacrifice, move directly toward the third-base line, halfway between the plate and third.

The first baseman should be in, ready to cover his side and the front of the mound.

If you can field the ball pivot to your gloved side and throw to his chest height, just on the infield side of the bag. The third baseman should be almost pointing to you with his glove.

STARTING THE DOUBLE PLAY

Again, if the shortstop and second baseman don't tell you who's covering second on a ball to the mound, ask them. Your timing has to be right to bring the ball to the base at the same time the fielder gets there. Give the ball to the fielder just slightly—a foot at most—on his side of the base, right at his chest. You want to give him a chance to have the ball before he reaches the bag and has to avoid a sliding runner.

COVERING FIRST BASE

Make it an automatic thing. Any time a ball is hit to your left side, your first reaction should be toward covering first base. Make it an automatic reaction, like saying "Good morning" to your parents at the breakfast table. The catcher should automatically yell for you to get over there. You can tell him you want to be reminded. If you're pitching a tough game, you often have to be reminded because you're concentrating so much on pitching. You can't forget those other things, or they'll cost you dearly.

If the first baseman can make the play, he'll wave you away. If not, keep coming. Run a straight line to a point about two steps on the plate side of the base, turn and go up the base line. You don't want to take the toss and then cross the bag in front of the runner. Keep yourself in fair territory, and you won't have the runner coming up your back.

52

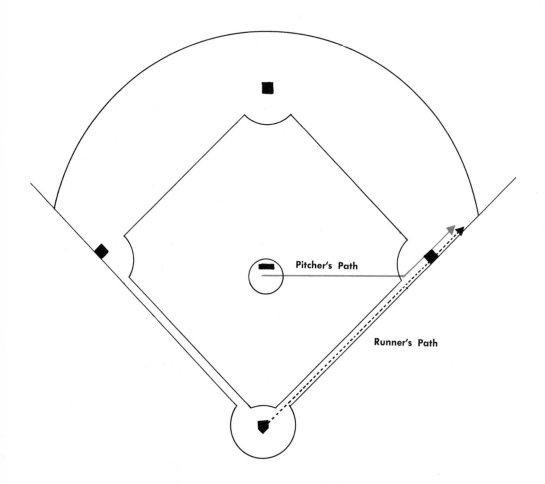

Pitcher's Path

Runner's Path

When you cover first base, run a straight line to a
point about two steps in front of the base, then turn
and run along the baseline to take the toss. Don't
cut in front of the runner.

In the 1969 World Series I was late getting there for a throw
from Donn Clendenon. I ran straight to the bag and ended up
cutting in front of Elrod Hendricks and getting spiked on the back
of my foot. If you make the play properly, you step on the top of
the infield edge of the bag.

53

Since the length of the throw from the first baseman isn't very great, it will usually be a soft throw. Those don't stick in your glove very well. Catch it with two hands. For that matter all balls should be caught with two hands whenever possible.

The slow-hit ball just between the pitcher and the first baseman can be a swift pain in the neck. It is your responsibility to call, "I have it" or "You take it." If the first baseman has to field the ball, you have to get to first base to take his throw. Try to tell him as soon as possible if you can make the play so he can get back to cover. On some occasions you will have to field the ball and continue with it to first base. Do it as if you were taking a throw, cutting up the line in fair territory.

BACKING UP THE THROW

You're an infielder, too, remember. Before the pitch you have to anticipate where the play is going to be and be there to back up the throw. If the ball is hit to left-center and there's a possibility of a play at either home or third base, cross the baseline between those two points so you can move wherever the ball goes. Get as far back as possible, not just six feet behind the third baseman or catcher. Often the ball is deflected to a new direction and you'll really have to move to save a run or an extra base.

When you're tired, these are hard things to do, but these are things winning pitchers do no matter how tired. If you know which runners are fast, it'll help you anticipate which base your fielders are likely to throw to.

Every player must anticipate the possible plays. Physical errors will happen, but most mental errors can be eliminated by forethought.

On a wild pitch or a passed ball with a runner on third, your job is to get home before the runner does. It's a very delicate play and hopefully you'll get a good throw from the catcher—and you catch it. The runner is going to come home sliding. Your job is to tag him on the ankles—get your glove in and out again as quickly as possible. Tag with the back of the glove. Get out of the way.

The pitcher has no protection except his own quickness. Once, when I was 15 years old, I made a tag and got my left arm deeply cut. I dropped the ball and needed eighteen stitches, too. It was my first look inside the human body.

HOLDING RUNNERS CLOSE

The key to preventing runners from taking a big lead is always the threat of a pickoff. Even if you haven't developed a deceptive pickoff move, the major rule is to make a good throw. We'll get into this more deeply in the next section, on the mechanics of pitching.

THE OFFENSIVE PITCHER

I'm not about to begin to try to make hitters out of pitchers who can't hit. For one thing, hitting is such a difficult art it's unreasonable to think that just because a man can pitch well, he should be able to hit well. There are very few men who can teach hitting.

But there are things a pitcher can do to help himself. He can know the strike zone when he's at bat. He knows how nice it is when he's pitching and the batter swings at a pitch that isn't a strike. Don't give the opposing pitcher help by swinging at bad balls.

And a pitcher—if he's any kind of athlete at all—can make himself a good bunter. It's something you have to be able to do.

The better bunter you are, the better your chances of winning your game. You can keep yourself in a game instead of going out for a pinch hitter if you know how to advance a runner. If you take batting practice and your share is ten swings, take two or three bunts.

55

Some coaches prefer the batter
to square his whole body
around to face the pitcher.
The bat is held the same in
either style.

Some coaches say square around to bunt, moving both feet
so you face the pitcher. I believe the best way is to pivot out of
your normal batting stance, rotating at the hips and turning on the
balls of both feet. Flex your knees a bit, and slide your top hand
up to the label on the bat or possibly a little higher.

56

My favorite bunting form has the batter in his normal
batting stance, rotating at the hips so that the
upper part of his body faces the pitcher.

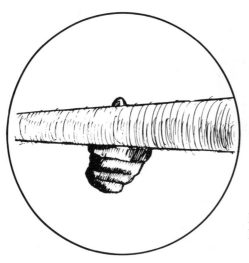

Note position of fingers when
bunting the ball.

Pinch the bat with your thumb and curl your fingers so they
aren't wrapped around the bat. Keep the bat up and out in front
of your body so you can see the ball actually make contact. Let
the ball hit the bat, don't push the bat at the ball. You want the
ball to come off slowly. Hold the bat firmly, but don't squeeze it.

The bunt. Pivot on the balls
of both feet from your batting
stance. Rotate at the hips so
the upper part of your body
faces the pitcher.
(Joe De Maria photo)

58

Grip for the bunt. See how the bottom hand is slid up just a bit for balance, but the top hand is up to the label. Pinch the bat with the thumb and first finger out of the way of the ball. *(Joe De Maria photo)*

And remember, your job on a sacrifice is to give yourself up. Don't begin to think about running to first base until the ball is down on the ground. After crossing first ease up gradually rather than stopping abruptly. It will save your legs.

If you're trying to advance a man to second base, try to angle your bat so the bunt goes up the first-base line. If you want to get

an help yourself by learn-
bunt. It takes practice
the ball down as shown
hen the Pirates are try-
make if difficult.
hoto)

When you get a turn in batting practice, make the
most of it; even in a borrowed jersey. *(UPI photo)*

the man to third, as we mentioned earlier, the intention is to make
the third baseman field the ball.

If you want to bunt a man to second in the eighth inning of a
tied game, that can be the winning run. It's worth practicing.

Try to help yourself as a hitter, too. So you can't make
yourself a Johnny Bench, you can make yourself as good a
hitting-pitcher as Tom Seaver. I work at it. I think it's a valuable
asset. Learn to get your bat on the ball. Learn to lose that natural
fear of the ball. Good hitters aren't afraid when you're pitching to
them.

There's plenty to time just lying around during practice. Ask
the coach if you and another pitcher or a couple of pitchers can
play pepper. If there's a batting cage going unused, ask if you can
use it. It will help you and the team.

You don't expect to be a hitter just because you're a pitcher, but you can help yourself by not swinging at bad pitches. *(UPI photo)*

The better hitter you are, the more you're going to help yourself. If the eighth hitter in the lineup hits a double and you can hit a ball on the ground to the right side so the runner advances to third, you've helped yourself as a pitcher.

RUNNING THE BASES

I love running the bases. One of the saddest parts of this game to me is that I don't get to play every day and run the bases like the regulars. Know when to go from first to third on a single and when not to. Know when taking a base on a borderline wild pitch is worth the risk.

Consider if you have a big lead, and it's a hot day. I

remember Steve Renko pitching for Montreal against us; he had a 9-1 lead. He hit a ball on the ground in the eighth inning and hustled all the way to first, but he couldn't make it through the ninth inning with his pitching even though he had that big lead. What was the value of first base—whether he was safe or out—then?

Of course, if the game is close and your extra base could mean something, then you are a baseball player, not just a pitcher. The coach has the play in front of him at all times. You don't. Let him tell you what to do. If you're on second base and the ball is hit to right field, your eyes should be on the third base coach, not the ball. He will tell you to continue around third or hold up.

SLIDING

Learn an efficient, simple way to slide. You want to get to the base as quickly as possible, stop on the base, and not get hurt. Learn the bent-leg slide.

When you get on base, pick up some dirt in each hand. That serves as a good reminder to keep your hands up and out of the way when you slide. Visualize a spot ten to fifteen feet before the base. That's your takeoff point. Fold one leg—pick whichever one is most natural for you—behind the other knee. Raise the straight leg enough to clear the ground—about six inches. Lean back and ride across the ground on the upper part of your thigh, the seat of your pants, and the lower part of your back.

Practice sliding on grass with a pair of Bermuda shorts under your uniform for protection. The grass will let you slide without much of a beating. The grass stains will also tell you where you're touching down.

Most important: When you decide to slide, do it. If you've decided to slide but the coach tells you to stand up or the next hitter tells you to come home standing up—you slide. The worst thing you can do is change your mind in midslide.

Jim Lefebvre of the Dodgers was coming home against the Twins in the 1965 World Series and halfway down from third was set to slide. Then the on-deck hitter held up his hands that Lefebvre could stand up, and he changed his mind. Somewhere in his indecision he hurt his knee and missed the entire next season. He hurt himself because he changed his mind.

GETTING HURT

Somewhere along the line you're going to catch a hard ground ball on your shins. A ball will bounce over your glove and hit you on the inside of your forearm. A pitched ball will hit you someplace and be painful. You'll rub the skin off your hip on a slide. It's a fact of life. You can also fall down your front steps and break your leg.

If you're consciously afraid of getting hurt, you're going to hurt yourself as a ballplayer. If you're in the correct stance after throwing the ball, you can protect yourself adequately on the mound—even if the ball does come back hard.

If you're afraid of the ball, you know it. Take ground balls, play pepper. If you're not a good fielder, work at it. Once you've practiced and developed a protective follow-through, you'll learn not to be afraid.

Nobody can tell you not to be afraid and make you not afraid. It doesn't work that way, ever. You have to convince yourself.

I feel that playing ball to the utmost of your ability is like going a hundred miles an hour under full control. It's not going with reckless abandon. Peter Reiser might have been considered one of the finest ball players of all time, but thirty years ago he played with reckless abandon. He left his enormous talent plastered against concrete outfield walls. It's like the line from the Broadway musical *Man of La Mancha*: "Whether the rock hits the pitcher (in this case a water pitcher) or the pitcher hits the rock, it's bound to be bad for the pitcher."

63

When you're playing out of control, running after a ball or whatever, you can normally expect to get hurt. You don't know exactly what you're doing.

When you do know what you're doing and playing in control, you're not going to get hurt often. Put it out of your mind.

6

Throwing the Ball

Once you've learned to handle yourself on the baseball field as a player, on offense and defense, you can begin to concentrate on getting the batters out. That's what pitching is all about. In the final analysis—the coach will put you out there on the mound because he thinks you can get the other side out better than somebody else.

Your body is in shape, you're confident you can handle a ball hit back to you, and you can cover first base. Now you get into throwing the ball.

To try to simplify things let's break this down into two sections. In this chapter we'll restrict ourselves to just throwing the ball: Developing an efficient motion from the time you take the sign from the catcher until the sound of your grunt fades away and you're in your follow-through.

We'll get into throwing the various pitches in the next chapter.

The primary objective on each pitch is to get all the physical and mental energies going toward home plate. You're not thinking about the error that's been made, the bad pitch you just threw, or how you're going to handle the hitter on deck. The only thought in your mind is the one pitch you're going to throw right now. If you're concentrating deeply, you won't even be conscious of any thought at all.

It's right there where you test your concentration and your

65

confidence. If you're still mulling over in your mind which pitch to throw, your mind is in the wrong place. If you're wondering if you can throw that pitch well enough, then go back three steps.

You begin the whole process by warming up. You're going to be pitching from a mound in a game so find a mound to use whenever you throw. The difference in your stride on a flat surface and on a mound can be all the difference in the world. I sometimes used the back of the high jump pit as a practice mound when I was in high school.

I prefer a warmup at full pitching distance. Some pitchers like to start at forty feet or so and gradually work back to sixty feet as their muscles loosen. That's fine, but make sure you start off at the mound and have your catcher back up toward the plate. Stay on that rubber all the time. Use each pitch to get your rhythm. Don't waste the warmups.

Once you're ready and the game begins, each sequence begins with taking the sign from the catcher—or actually a moment before the catcher gives the sign. Unless the coach or manager has strict instructions that the catcher calls the game or that all the pitches will be called from the bench, the ultimate decision is up to the pitcher. He has to throw the ball. To think the catcher called for the wrong pitch in a critical situation is a cop-out, a lame excuse.

The sign is to help the catcher handle the pitch, so he knows what's coming.

HOLDING AND HIDING THE BALL

The last few years a style of pitching has evolved that to an extent has simplified pitching. Back when Don Larsen pitched his perfect game against the Dodgers in the 1956 World Series, it was a significant observation that he used a "no-windup" delivery. Actually, he did use a windup. There's no way developed so far that enables a pitcher to throw without a windup. But Larsen didn't use the flowing, pumping style of windup that was in wide use then.

He used a short, compact windup that many pitchers—including myself—and pitching coaches now think is more effective for building control and staying power. It's a very orthodox style now, and I'm a rather orthodox pitcher. That's clear to anybody who's ever hit against me or watched me pitch. It's like the way Vince Lombardi coached football: You're not likely to get anything you don't expect against me. But I'll try to throw a pitch when you don't expect it and to make it such a good pitch that even if you were expecting it, you couldn't handle it.

I don't believe in a lot of trickery or freak action on the mound. The time it takes to develop that sort of thing would be better spent perfecting sound basic equipment.

It's almost impossible to teach someone to throw a ball by putting words on paper. It's like trying to describe a giraffe to someone who's never seen one. You learn to throw by seeing other people throw and then experimenting by yourself. There are basic elements common to everyone, but the rhythm of shifting weight and balance comes by feel. Others can only make suggestions.

It used to be general thinking that a pitcher had to throw every pitch the same way—same grip and so on. I never could understand that thinking. Each pitch is supposed to do something different, so you find the way to make each pitch do what it's supposed to. You try to make each pitch look the same to the batter until it's too late to make a difference to him.

You don't want him to know what's coming in time for him to adjust his timing and swing. You want him to see the ball as little as possible until you release it. Even if he knows where the ball is, his anticipation will be a little behind.

Taking the Sign. Take your stance with your right foot on the rubber (assuming you're right-handed as I am. If you're left-handed, reverse the instructions.) and your left a comfortable half-step ahead. Your front spikes should be over the front edge of the rubber.

67

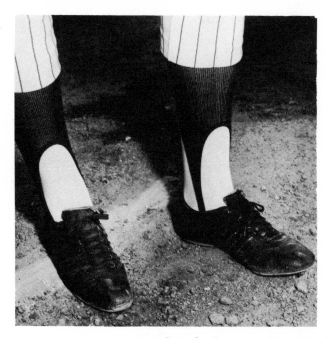

Start your delivery here, taking the sign from the catcher. The right foot straddles the rubber. *(Joe De Maria photo)*

Stand where you're going to make the pitch. I prefer to pitch off the right side of the rubber, because it emphasizes the angle at which the ball travels to the batter. My arm is at the right side of my body. Remember to use the same place on the rubber for every pitch. If you change places for certain pitches, the hitters will learn to read that quick enough the way they learned that

The ball is in your glove, seams correctly positioned for the pitch. *(Joe De Maria photo)*

Babe Ruth, when he was a pitcher, stuck out his tongue when he threw a curveball.

Have the ball in the palm of your glove in front of you as you read the sign. Hold it at your waist or at your chest, any comfortable position. The ball should be already set so you can reach in and grip it properly as you begin to swing into your delivery. That way you can get your grip without fumbling around in the glove, and the glove will mask the ball until you're about to make it disappear behind your body. Once the ball begins to move it's too late to read the pitch from your grip. If the hitter is busy trying to see that, he's not concentrating enough on his own job.

The important thing is to have the heel of your pitching hand in the same place as you take the ball out of the glove. You can't reach in from the bottom for the fastball and from the side for a curve.

THE MOTION

There are three basic types of pitching delivery and countless variations in between: overhand, three-quarters, and sidearm. Think of standing at the plate and visualizing a big clock on the mound. When a right-handed pitcher reaches up to eleven or twelve o'clock, he's throwing overhand. When he comes through ten, that's three-quarters; nine or eight-thirty is sidearm.

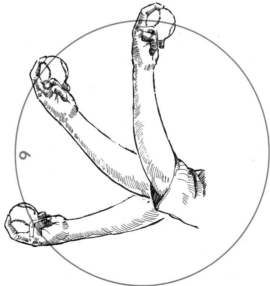

Visualize a big clock on the mound. When a right-hander delivers the ball from 11 or 12 o'clock, he's throwing overhand. About 10 o'clock is three-quarters and 9 or 8 is sidearm.

Three-quarter motion. The
wrist is above the elbow.
(Joe De Maria photo)

A few pitchers deliver the ball below that, but not many.
That's underhand or submarine, and it's effective for a while
because hitters see that motion so seldom. But there's a strong
restriction on what you can do with a ball and a loss of velocity
from that motion. Hitters quickly learn to take advantage of that.

Overhand. Generally if your elbow is above your shoulder,
you're pitching overhand. Sandy Koufax was an overhand pitcher.
I prefer to pitch that way, over the top of my body. I believe that
enables you to take full advantage of the weight of your body to
lean into the pitch, and it gives your arm a greater arc at the point
of release. You have more leverage, and you can get the best
rotation on a curveball. Hitters usually feel most comfortable

70

against overhand pitchers. There's less difference to left-handed or right-handed hitters, because the ball doesn't come at as much angle.

Three-Quarters. If your elbow is even with your shoulder and your wrist above your elbow, call it three-quarters. Bob Gibson is a three-quarters pitcher. Don Drysdale and Ferguson Jenkins look like sidearmers because they're so tall and reach out so far, but at the point of release they still have the wrist above the elbow. I don't think you can get quite as good break on a curveball three-quarters as you can overhand, but you do get more angle on the hitter.

Sidearm. The greatest advantage a pitcher has against a hitter hitting from the same side is demonstrated by a sidearmer. Take a tall fellow like lefty Steve Hamilton—six feet, seven inches and appropriately long arms—reaching all the way out to pitch: A

Overhand motion. The elbow is above the shoulder.

Sidearm motion. Shoulder, elbow and wrist on the same plane. *(Joe De Maria photos)*

left-handed hitter must think the first baseman is throwing the ball. He was a devastating relief pitcher to left-handed hitters. Gil Hodges used to kid about how hard it was for a right-hander to hit against Ewell Blackwell in the 1940s. But there aren't many sidearm pitchers around now in the twenty-game category. The advantage on one side becomes a disadvantage on the other. It's very difficult to get good downward break on a curveball for a sidearmer.

And then there's a fellow like Juan Marichal who can throw four pitches from each of those motions and make a hitter think the man has a dozen pitches that all work.

Because I prefer overhand, don't think that's one of the rules of the game. I think the overhand delivery offers advantages, but the first rule of pitching is to get the hitter out. You find out what works best for you. Experiment. Try different things. Try your pitches from various deliveries in batting practice or on the sidelines, and see how the hitters react. That's the best indication you'll find.

THE BACKSWING

The first half of your windup is getting yourself ready to throw the pitch. The objective is to get your hand out of the glove with the ball and to a position to begin the forward motion of your body and the ball. It's drawing back the string of a powerful bow.

You want your backswing to be comfortable and free, but you want it to be compact. You want your energies going on a straight line to the plate. You don't want your arms and legs all over the place. There are herky-jerky pitchers around, but you'll find the best pitchers usually have smooth deliveries in which effort isn't wasted.

Take your stance on the rubber, right shoe extended over the front of the rubber and left foot a bit ahead. Take a half-stride backward with your left foot, and your hands will come up

When you reach into the glove it should be simple to pick up the correct grip and begin to swing into the backswing. *(Joe De Maria photo)*

Your hands start up, your left foot comes back, and your weight is shifted back behind the rubber. *(Joe De Maria photo)*

naturally over your head. The ball is still in your glove, out of the batter's sight. Your eyes are fixed on the catcher's target. The balance of your body shifts slightly onto the back foot.

Then your hands separate for the first time. Do it quickly, briskly. Get the ball out of your glove, and get it up. That's the peak of your backswing. Your muscles are coiled.

I'll repeat: Get it out, and get it up. You can't dawdle here

73

The moment of poise. Your
weight is over the rubber and
just beginning to flow into
the forward swing of your kick.
(Joe De Maria photo)

The peak of the backswing, just
before the ball starts forward.
Your left toes are reaching
forward and your wrist is
cocked. *(Joe De Maria photo)*

and draw the ball back. Get it out, and get it up.

If you're lazy coming out of the glove, you'll be late coming
down with the ball, and your pitches will be high. It takes only a
fraction of a second delay to prevent you from keeping the ball
down.

To be a successful pitcher at any level, you have to keep the
74   ball down. To keep it down consistently you've got to get the ball
out of the glove and get it up.

The moment the ball comes out of your glove and your hands separate, your weight has shifted to your right foot on the rubber and you are lifting your left leg and moving it toward the plate.

Your leg reaches the highest point of the kick and reaches forward. Your hand has taken the ball to the deepest point of the backswing. The instant before the left toe touches down, the arm has gone back as far as it's going to go and the hand with the ball reaches back a tiny bit more. That's where the wrist is cocked. The timing here is delicate as a good watch. You must work on that rhythm constantly.

There are a number of pitchers who draw the ball back behind the right leg, almost scraping it on the mound behind them. I think that's an inefficient delivery, hard to control. The ball has to be moved too far from the peak of the backswing to the point of release. The momentum your arm builds for most of that distance is valueless. It increases the degree of error, and all of the motion is intended to concentrate the effort in a distance of about a foot of motion before the release.

I believe in keeping the elbow bent and the ball high. That's more compact and, I believe, a more controlled delivery. It also helps you with runners on base, as we'll discuss later.

At precisely the break of the backswing, the point where your arm goes back no farther, there's a momentary pause, a hesitation you hardly see. It's like flipping a coin into the air and watching it reach the top and start down. You know it stopped at the peak, but it was so brief you couldn't see it.

TOWARD THE PLATE

That's where the backswing becomes the forward movement. At the instant the forward movement begins, you cock your wrist. Your hand lays back at the wrist, the ball firm in the fingers. It's as if your hand were reaching for a little more backswing while your arm has started forward.

75

Your leg has reached the maximum height of your kick, your wrist is cocked, and you begin to reach forward with your gloved hand. That arm should be coiled rather than extended.

The purpose of the kick is to get you into position to deliver the ball. You put your weight into a balance, and then you go forward. It's the final thing that happens before you start your forward momentum. You find your own most effective style. Don't think you have to kick the sky, don't try to copy someone else because he looks good. Find something that works for you.

When your leg starts down, you're driving toward the plate. You're starting to deliver the ball.

Everything you've been doing until this point has been with your pitching side. When you begin to reach forward with the gloved hand, you begin to employ the other side of your body. Your left side begins to move toward the plate, and it's as if there were a link between your gloved hand and your chest.

Your forward foot makes contact with the mound, the ball of the foot first, the knee flexed as a shock absorber. You lean your weight into that front leg. The ball is being delivered as all

Often when you lean into a pitch, you'll touch the mound with your knee. *(UPI photo)*

your energy is flowing into that front leg. Then you seem to be pulling your body around with that link between your gloved hand and your chest.

All this time your eyes are on the target.

Now your left side begins to open toward the plate. Your left knee opens, your hip, and your shoulder. As the left side turns, your right side comes forward. You're pushing with your right foot on the rubber.

The ball is passing your ear at that time. Your knee is closed, your hip is closed, your shoulder is closed, and suddenly they open. Boom—it comes.

Again your gloved hand is never behind your body. It must be even with the front half of your body or in front of it for balance and self-protection. It takes too long to get it from behind you to handle a hard-hit ball.

This is the last moment of coiled muscles before the ball is released. There's a puff of dirt where the back foot is pushing off, the knee is almost in the dirt. The ball is coming to the point where the muscles suddenly drive it toward the batter. This fastball was pitched the night we beat the Pirates 1-0, for my 20th victory in 1972. *(UPI photo)*

77

Follow-through. The ball has already left your hand when you follow through, so it has no effect on the flight of the ball. But everything you do after you release the ball is a result of what you do before the release. If you don't follow through, then you've begun to slow your arm to its stop too soon.

Bend at the waist. Let the momentum of your hand carry it across in front of your body. Let the end of the motion come gradually rather than in an abrupt, pushing jerk.

When you get the whole sequence going right, you'll notice other things. When you're leaning completely into the pitch, you may notice that your right knee may brush the mound as you release the ball, that the instep of your right shoe scrapes across the mound. Then you're extending your leg and driving into the pitch. Nelson Briles occasionally leans so hard into his fastball that he throws himself onto his belly on the mound.

At the peak of my delivery, at the moment I take the ball out of my glove and get it up to the top of the arc, I dip into my right leg just an instant. For me that acts as another bit of coiling before I drive forward.

But that's my style. Find your own.

The follow-through. Note how all the weight has shifted to the front foot. The rear foot is just being pulled away from its contact with the rubber. *(AP photo)*

Note here how the instep drags away from the rubber
and the knee brushes the dirt as the body is braced
against the planted left leg. *(UPI photo)*

Leaning into a pitch against the Phillies. Notice
how the camera has picked up the stitches of the
rotating ball, but my pitching hand was still moving
in a blurr. *(UPI photo)*

STRETCH MOTION

You don't want baserunners taking advantage of you, but you can't forget that your primary job is to deliver the baseball to the plate. You can't do anything that will detract from that. You can't shorten your motion just because runners are on base. Work out a delivery you can use equally with runners on and with bases empty. In this way your delivery will always be the same.

Getting there is somewhat different. A left-handed pitcher has the advantage with runners on first base because he's naturally looking that way. Lefties and righties are even with a runner on second, and the righty has the edge at third—but you shouldn't have too many runners on third. Unless you're expecting a squeeze play or a ball deliberately tapped on the ground, you usually won't use a stretch motion with a runner on third.

Start by taking the sign with the outside of your right foot in contact with the front of the rubber. Have the ball in position in your glove. You face third base with your left shoulder pointed to

Stance with runners on base. Make contact with the rubber with the side of your right foot. Your toes should be at the same location on the rubber as in your regular delivery. (Joe De Mario photo)

80

the plate. Bring your hands together in front of your body at a comfortable position and get your grip on the ball. You must make a distinct pause there, standing straight up.

From that position you can look over your left shoulder to watch the runner on first. You can look at the plate or to first with little more than a shift of your eyes. You have to establish a routine that doesn't become a routine; otherwise the good baserunners will figure it out. Sometimes you look once, sometimes twice, and so on.

The intent is too keep the runner from getting too big a lead and to prevent him from getting a continuous walking lead. You have to make him stop. Sometimes you can make him stop just by looking at him. Sometimes you have to throw to first. Ideally you want the runner to think you're throwing to first when you're going to the plate and the other way around.

With your hands in front of your body, you can throw to the plate or spin and throw to first without changing your position. Most frequently you will raise your front foot as if throwing to the plate, then turn toward your gloved side pivoting on the foot next to the rubber. Concentrate on making a good throw to first base—knee high over the base. If you throw the ball into right field, have you held the runner close?

Occasionally you'll want to throw to first from another position, perhaps before you've come to the set with the ball in front of your body. You actually jump off the ground enough to turn both feet around and throw to first. It's a quick snap throw.

A left-hander has the runner in front of him. He can lift his leg as if throwing home and stride toward first instead.

With a runner on first, the pitcher may not fake a throw while he has his foot on the rubber. The pitcher must step in the direction of his throw—he can't step to the plate and throw to first. That's called a balk, and the runner is moved to second.

You must make the runner come to a stop. Good stealers have great timing, and you don't want them already moving toward the next base when you release the ball to the plate. You have to give your catcher a chance to throw the man out.

Ray Sadecki once threw to first base seventeen times to make Maury Wills stop. Wills refused to stop, and eventually Sadecki picked him off. In the 1972 World Series, Blue Moon Odom threw to first base seven consecutive times to make Joe Morgan stop. When Odom did throw to the plate, Morgan broke for second, but he was either worn down from all the diving back to first or had taken a shorter lead than he planned. The catcher threw him out. There is also the risk that the pitcher will get worn down or throw the ball away. Remember your primary job is to get the ball to the plate.

A pickoff to second is more complicated. We'll get to that in a later chapter.

A basic rule to remember is that you can do almost anything you want with the ball if you have your foot off the rubber. If the runner or a possible play has you confused, step off the rubber. Then you're an infielder. Say you're in a set position with your foot on the rubber and you turn and run after the runner, it's a balk. However, if you take your foot off the rubber first, you can chase him.

FINDING THE FLAWS

The best way to find out what you're doing wrong is to have someone who knows about pitching watch you closely. If you have a videotape replay machine in your home, that's wonderful. But who does? Have another pitcher watch you. Practice your motion in front of a full-length mirror.

Look for these basic mistakes.

Hard Landing. Come down from your kick smoothly on the ball of your foot. When you land on your heel, you jolt your body and you throw high.

(You may notice that most of these flaws cause you to throw the ball high. High pitches are either out of the strike zone and cause you to walk batters, or they're high in the strike zone and just where the hitter wants them. In either case it's not good for the pitcher.

Overstriding. Simply put, if you make contact with the ground with your front leg stiff, you're striding too far. That long stride tends to get your weight too far back. Try to keep your weight approximately over the rubber. If you get your weight too far back, your arm never catches up with your forward movement: You tend to throw high. That means your leading foot has already made contact, and your hand hasn't brought the ball to intended release point yet.

It's all just a matter of inches, but then the plate is only seventeen inches wide to begin with. That was Nolan Ryan's problem with the Mets. He'd get his weight way, way back. His arm couldn't catch up, and he'd be consistently high ith his pitches.

Rushing The Delivery. A pitcher trying to throw hard may get himself to the collection point of his motion—when he has his weight in the proper balance to take his stride—and then jerk himself into a rush. I do it sometimes, a lot of people do. It's a very common flaw. The point is that it's not the speed of your body that's important to a fastball. Making the body move fast doesn't make the ball go fast.

What gives you maximum velocity when the ball comes out of your hand is timing, getting all the parts of your body together. If you move your body too quickly, you've expended all your energy but haven't thrown the ball yet. When you do release it, there's nothing there. You're in a situation when you feel an urgency to throw hard, so you rush all the parts of your body and make nothing of your effort.

Overthrowing. This is a brother of rushing. It comes from that same feeling of urgency. You're trying to do more than you can. As hard as Nolan Ryan could throw when he wasn't half trying, he tried to throw even harder than that. A piece of advice I got from Harvey Haddix, our pitching coach when I was a rookie: Know yourself; know what you can do and try to perform as efficiently as you can at that level.

83

Shakespeare, an earlier pitching coach, said: "This above all, to thine own self be true." He meant, don't try to fool yourself. Don't try to do more than you can do. If you can't throw a ball as hard as Sandy Koufax, don't try to. You'll end up throwing not as hard as you can throw it. "Know yourself" is a good piece of advice.

Across the Body. Here's a little test you can apply to yourself. Draw a line in the dirt of the mound directly between your feet when you stand on the rubber to the plate. Go through your motion and see where your front foot lands. It should touch down on that line or slightly to the left, preferably slightly to the left. That stride will open up your body.

If your foot is touching down to the right of the line, you're throwing across your body. That means you're throwing with your arm and making very little use of the power of the rest of your body. That's a common problem with sidearm pitchers. They step to the right and throw across the body. That puts a lot of strain on the arm.

Don Drysdale looked like a sidearm pitcher because he was so tall, but he took his stride straight ahead and reached out wide.

Drag Arm. This is a flaw that really isn't a flaw. With a drag-arm motion, the release is a fraction behind the impact of the foot. The front of the body is a little more opened at the time of release. Drag-arm pitchers don't throw the ball so much as they sling it. Joe Hoerner pitches that way. So did Ron Perranoski, and he was a top-level relief pitcher for a long time.

I don't think I'd try to change a drag-arm pitcher if he was most effective with that kind of motion and it didn't hurt him.

Advice. As long as you pitch, somebody is going to give you advice. Bob Shaw, now a pitching coach, joined our club when I was a rookie and cornered me. He tried to revise my style of pitching completely after seeing me for the extended period of ten days. I couldn't handle that. But one piece of advice I got from another veteran pitcher was that I was going to be innundated

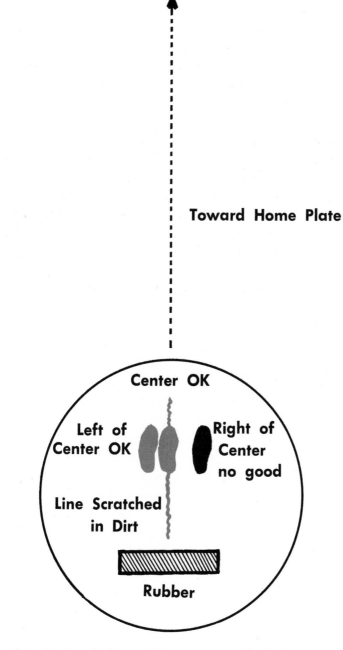

Toward Home Plate

Center OK

Left of
Center OK

Right of
Center
no good

Line Scratched
in Dirt

Rubber

Your force is reduced when you throw across your body.
Scratch a line on the mound between your feet toward
the plate. Go through your motion and note where
your front foot strikes. It should touch down slightly
to the left of the line or directly on it—certainly
not to the right.

85

with advice. He said, if it makes sense, try it. If then it doesn't work for you, forget it.

Don't get your back up and reject all advice. Why should you throw away a bit of advice that may help your whole career just because you're stubborn?

There are all kinds of ways to experiment. Dick Selma, who kept turning up on my team from high school days in Fresno, California, until the Mets, is a great experimenter. He's also proof of the idea that you can be strong even if you aren't big.

He had a different pitching theory every other week, and he'd like to test them all. He'd take one new idea to the pitching coach or to another pitcher and ask what they thought of it. Some of his theories he'd try in batting practice. And sometimes he couldn't wait that long.

One spring Dick roomed with Danny Frisella at the Colonial Inn, the Mets' headquarters in St. Petersburg, Florida. That spring Frisella, a thick-muscled fellow, brought a cast-iron ball from his home in San Francisco, a weight that was used on fishing nets. Frisella had filed off the ring, making it about the size of a baseball and very heavy.

Frisella and a number of pitchers like to use the weighted ball to stretch their muscles, holding the ball back over their shoulder and raising it up and down. That's why Frisella brought it. One afternoon Danny went to get his hair cut and when he got back, Dick was working out with the iron ball.

Dick had the pillows propped against the head of the bed on one side of the room, and he was on the other side working on his delivery. He was experimenting and getting exercise done at the same time.

Frisella opened the door and walked in just when Selma thought he was onto something good. "Watch this," Selma said and delivered the ball to the pillows.

But this time he missed the pillows and the head of the bed, and the ball went right through the wall to the next room. It made a nice round hole as if an artillery shell had passed through.

Danny and Dick experimented with the furniture in the

room, trying to rearrange the pieces so the chambermaid wouldn't find the hole. Finally, as a last resort, they hung a picture waist high, right over the hole. What else could they do?

When the chambermaid asked about the picture, Dick explained: "We like it better that way."

7

Making a Pitch

A few years ago there was considerable argument presented that a curveball really didn't curve, that it was all an optical illusion and a mystic power the devil gave to pitchers to cloud the mind of the batter. By the same token, a sinker didn't sink, a slider didn't slide, and a fastball didn't hop.

That argument has disappeared, and the fact of life of the movement of a pitch is thoroughly accepted. I certainly never heard of a hitter who said the ball didn't curve. The movement of the ball is baseball's ultimate weapon.

Good pitching stops good hitting. It's a very simple statement, and it's true. I know it. Every pitcher knows it and so does every realistic hitter. But there's one strong modifier: Good pitching succeeds—only if it's good enough. A great pitcher throws a pitch that's not quite so good or gets it in a bad place, and he becomes a bad pitcher. Then the statement becomes: Good hitting wrecks bad pitching.

It's the pitcher's job to make the theory work for him. He has to throw the pitch the hitter isn't expecting and make the ball do what he wants.

How many different pitches does a pitcher need? That's like asking how many oxtails would it take to make a rope that would reach the moon? The answer is: One—if it's long enough. The answer about the number of pitches is: One—if it's good enough.

But that's unrealistic. Even if that one pitch were a

superpitch, the hitter would be looking for it all the time and would take advantage of the slightest mistake.

And almost nobody can throw any one pitch that well. That remains to a Walter Johnson, Bobby Feller or Sandy Koufax. When they were at their peaks Johnson and Feller were great fastball pitchers. Koufax had a great fastball, but he also had a great curveball.

I remember the observation by Ralph Kiner, once among the best home-run hitters in baseball, that Koufax could beat you with his fastball alone or his curve alone. If he had both pitches working that game, it was an automatic three-hitter.

If the hitter had two pitches to look for, his job becomes so much harder. If he has to look for three pitches and they're all good pitches, then the pitcher's advantage is enormous.

The fastball is still the best pitch in baseball and no doubt always will be. But a pitcher should have a breaking ball of some sort—either a curveball or a slider—to be effective. In higher levels of competietion a third pitch is advisable. There's the fastball on one end of the scale, the curveball on the other. The slider is in between; it looks like the fastball, and it behaves something like the curve. Then what is the hitter to look for?

No, don't feel sorry for him yet. If you can also throw a good change of pace, a pitch that looks like your fastball and comes up not quite so fast, you can start to think: "poor hitter, too bad."

Fastball, curve, slider, and change of pace are the four basic pitches to be mastered. Almost all pitches fit one of these categories.

There are a few others. The sinker and screwball are effective but for only a few pitchers and they're very hard on the arm. They're best left for highly advanced pitchers. Most often they're used by pitchers as they get older and need to make up for a loss of speed. I consider the knuckleball, forkball, and palmball freak pitches or trick pitches. If they're easy for you to throw, not hard on your arm, and you can control them, go ahead and use them.

A really good knuckleball—like Hoyt Wilhelm's—is almost

unhittable. Sometimes it's also uncatchable. But how many pitchers have there ever been who could throw a good knuckleball and control it? Of approximately 240 pitchers in the big leagues, you might count five who throw a good knuckler. Bad knucklers get hit.

Basically, you're better off working on the standard pitches. The change is a very hard pitch to learn and takes a lot of work. And there are a number of doctors and coaches who feel that the curveball damages the arm of a boy under 16 or so.

Then that brings us back to our old friend the fastball, which always was the best pitch, anyhow.

The Fastball. If you have a good fastball, it makes every other pitch more effective. If the hitter has to be conscious of the fastball he can't look for the curve. And there's that constant power of the fastball.

It's rare that you can pitch with nothing but the fastball, but it happens. I've had games when nothing was working for me except the fastball. I had good velocity with it, good control, and it moved well, I used it for 80 to 100 of 120 pitches.

Physically the hitters weren't able to handle it. The ball was traveling at such speed that by the time the batter's mind was able to tell him to swing, where to swing, and when to swing, it was too late. By then the ball was past him, off the end of his bat, or on the handle.

Now consider that there are two kinds of fastball—a rising fastball and a sinking fastball. The velocity is important, but if most fastballs are straight the better hitters will handle them. The fastball has to move. When Bob Gibson throws his best fastball, it seems to explode as the hitter takes his swing. Nolan Ryan's fastball looks as if it's hitting something and jumping on the way to the plate.

The basic fastball grip is with the first two fingers spread about half an inch at the tips. Some pitchers spread a little more. The thumb is largely straight and under the ball. The ball is out in the fingers.

90

The difference between one fastball and the other is in the contact with the seams.

The Rising Fastball. Hold this one across the large seams with the pads of the first two fingers on the seam and the contact of the thumb underneath on the smooth surface. When you give the ball the last pop of your wrist at the end of your motion, the seam rolls off the tip of the middle finger.

That's the pitch that makes batters make flat-handed motions in the dressing room like fighter pilots describing a dogfight. Nolan Ryan throws it. That's what Vida Blue was throwing against the Tigers in the last game of the American League playoff in 1972. "The Tigers would have been better off without bats," said Pete Rose of the Red, who watched on television. "The ball was rising over their bats and right out of the strike zone. If they had taken the pitches, they'd have been called balls."

But at the moment the Tigers had to decide to swing, Blue's

Rising fastball grip. Fingers spread about a half-inch, placed across the wide seams, stitching under the pads of the fingers. *(Joe De Maria photo)*

91

pitches were headed for the strike zone. The good fastball doesn't give the hitter much time to make up his mind.

Sinking Fastball. Hold this one with the first two fingers along the narrow seams. The pad of the middle finger is in contact with the stitches, and the seam on the underside rests just inside the knuckle of your thumb.

So many of the things you do pitching you discover not quite by accident. You're not working on anything, but you're throwing the ball in the outfield and observing what happens when you do different things. I'm sure that's how Mickey Lolich learned to throw his fastball, which is different than either of mine. He holds the ball with his two fingers on the slick, broad surface of the ball without contact with the seams. The ball comes up spinning oddly and then sinks as if it were a spitter.

Sinking fastball. Fingers along the narrow seams, lower seam across the outer section of the thumb. *(Joe De Maria photo)*

Curveball. It's remarkable how many good hitters there are against pretty good fastballs who can't handle the curve. There are a lot of explanations for that. For one, the hitter must calculate the speed of the ball: How much it's going to curve, and how much it's going to drop in order for him to know where it's going to be when he swings.

That's difficult in itself. Then there's always the factor of fear, and you shouldn't put that out of your mind. A good right-handed curve looks as if it's going to hit a right-handed hitter before it breaks over the plate. If the hitter flinches away from the ball for an instant, he won't be able to hit it after it breaks.

There is a common misunderstanding of the curve among young players. They don't realize that a good curve breaks down as well as across. It must if it's going to be effective. It's much more difficult to make a sidearm curve break downward.

But if you throw a good sidearm fastball, learn to throw a sidearm curve or a slider. Every place you throw a fastball, you should throw a breaking ball, or the hitters will read what you're throwing.

You try to make the ball rotate as rapidly as possible when it comes out of your hand. That's what makes it break. Don't get discouraged if you find it a difficult pitch to learn. It takes many pitchers years to learn to throw it.

Hold the ball along the seams, with your two fingers spread a little, or together if it's more comfortable. The pads on the tips of the fingers are extended just beyond the stitches. Your thumb is bent slightly, and the fleshy part of the thumb is in contact with the ball.

Try to get the ball coming off the edge of the index finger; you want the pressure on the ball from the middle finger and the thumb. Hold it firm so you can almost hear a pop when the ball comes out, but don't squeeze. The ball is deeper in the hand than the grip on the fastball.

When I take the ball to the top of my backswing, the curve looks exactly the same as the fastball except for the grip. When I

93

Curveball. A view from the plate as the ball passes the pitcher's ear. Fingers are along the seam and over the ball in preparation for pulling downward. *(Joe De Maria photo)*

start forward, the distinction begins. My hand and wrist begin to fold, so I can get my hand over the ball in the delivery. The palm is turned in toward the body rather than facing the plate.

You try to get as much of your fingers over the ball as possible. Then you make a downward snap of your hand and wrist. Keep your elbow above your shoulder to get as big an arc with your hand as possible. Pull down as hard as you can.

Remember, a sideward motion will produce a flat curve. The downward motion produces the curve that breaks in that deceptive combination of down and across. And again, remember, you want as much rotation as possible.

When Sandy Koufax was throwing his best overhand curve-ball, it was breaking downward as much as four feet. Just imagine a hitter at the plate waiting for a Koufax pitch.

The ball is chest high. If it's a fastball, the hitter knows it will jump up around his neck. If it's a curve, it will break down across his shins. The hitter has to decide which it is. When I'm throwing my curve well, I can expect three feet of downward break and eighteen inches laterally.

You'll have to work out how hard to throw the curve for yourself. You want to throw it as hard as you can and still enable the ball to break the maximum. The emphasis is on the snap and rotation more than on speed.

You want maximum velocity, but if you get velocity, great rotation, and the ball never has time to break, what do you have? You have a sixty-five-foot curve and the distance to the plate is sixty feet.

Then you have to back off on the speed just a little bit to give the curve a chance to break. Some times it feels like Humphrey Bogart's explanation in *Beat the Devil*, of how the English grow such fine lawns: "Give it plenty of water and roll it every day for 300 years." It takes some pitchers seven, eight, or ten years to get it right.

I think a slow curve is even more difficult to throw. You have

95

to reduce the velocity but maintain the rotation. But it's awfully nice to make a hitter in a breaking-ball situation worry about whether it'll be a hard curve or a slow one. It requires a great sense of touch to throw it well. I can do it only on good days.

Keep this in mind: Although we'll discuss placement and pitch selection in the next chapter, all curveballs should be thrown from the batter's waist down. You'll get better rotation on the ball if you can hold it the instant longer it takes to throw the ball down. You can lean into the pitch better when you're throwing low. And it's much harder for the hitter to hit a low curveball.

The Slider. Lurking somewhere in between the fastball and the curve is the slider, probably the most important weapon the pitcher has developed in the last twenty years. It breaks too much for the hitter to look for a fastball, and it travels too fast for him to look for a curve. It doesn't break very much—perhaps five inches across and two inches down—but it breaks very late.

It's the pitch that right-handed hitters think is down the middle but slides over the outside corner, the one that breaks the bat of the left-handed hitter.

The closest relative of the pitch is what used to be called a "nickle curve," which was really just a curve that didn't break very much. The slider today is much more refined. Few pitchers throw both a good curve and a good slider. Bob Gibson throws a fine slider. Koufax never had one but he had the great curve.

The grip is similar to the curveball, but the ball is farther out in the fingers. (The fastball is at the tips, the curve is deep in the hand, and the slider is in between.) Hold the ball along the broad seams again, but the slider is thrown with a quick rotation of the wrist at the end of the delivery rather than the big motion that begins at the top of the backswing.

Consider the ball at arm's length; visualize it as the face of a clock. When you come through on a fastball, your fingers are at twelve o'clock. On a slider your fingers are at two o'clock.

You deliver the ball as if it were a fastball, and at the latest point of release you pop your wrist down from two o'clock. Ah, the hitter will hate you.

Slider. Ball held slightly off-center to the pitcher's right, two fingers together, middle finger on the seam. *(Joe De Maria photo)*

Back to our old friend the clock. (A) On a fastball you want to grip the ball directly on top, as at midnight—or noon. (B) For a slider, hold it a little off-center, as at 2 o'clock.

A.

B.

Now you have a fastball that moves up or down, a curveball, and the slider that looks like both at the same time. After mastering one more pitch, you can go directly to the Hall of Fame. You need a pitch that looks as if it's a fastball but doesn't get to the plate until the batter has already spent the force of his swing.

The Change of Pace. The basic theory of pitching involves spoiling the hitter's sense of timing. That's what the change of pace is intended to do. Say you throw the big three—fastball, slider, and curve—and they're all thrown hard; then you can drop in a slow curve or a change-up. Beautiful. Then when you've shown the hitter he has to think about a change, it makes your other pitches more effective.

The change is a very hard pitch to learn, and it takes a lot of work. You may find it's more to your benefit to put the change off for another day. I've had a lot of difficulty learning it, but there are days when things are going so right that the change is right along with the other pitches.

The basic thing to understand is that it's not a "slowball." It isn't slow at all; it's something off a fastball. You don't want it to be so slow that the hitter has time to take his false stride and then regoup himself for a well-timed swing. You want the ball to zip in there just after he's set his stroke for a fastball. Then it's too late for him to change, and he's already committed the energy of his bat.

Some pitchers choke the ball deep in their fingers to reduce velocity. Some hold it entirely in the palm. Ferguson Jenkins spreads his first two fingers to hold the ball in a kind of fork (as in the pitch known as the forkball). He finds he can make his hard motion, and the ball doesn't go very hard. By dragging my right foot on the relese, I try to hold the ball an instant longer than on my fastball.

Find out which method works for you, but the key to a change is control. You have to be able to put the ball where you want it. Like most of the other pitches, you want the change low.

99

Change-up. The ball is deep in the hand, fingertips not in contact. The ball is clasped by the thumb and inner parts of the fingers. *(Joe De Maria photo)*

A theory I learned in college is that a change on the knees is one hundred percent effective. You've upset the hitter's sense of timing, and you've thrown a strike. A change below the knees is fifty percent effective. You've disturbed his timing, as intended; even though you didn't get a strike the ball was below the dangerous hitting area. You haven't lost anything.

8

Be a Pitcher

The higher you go as a pitcher the more you learn that your body isn't the only thing that gets tired in a close game. I can pitch nine innings, win 9-1, and feel as if I haven't pitched at all. It was an easy game. Then I can pitch the same nine innings in a 2-1 game, exert the same physical effort, and be totally exhausted when it's over. The great drain is really in the head.

That's where you stop being a thrower and begin to be a pitcher. Your arm may lose a little of its zip as you get older, but you're supposed to make up for it with your head. Make your own equation: Being a winning pitcher is 50 percent arm and 50 percent head. Or maybe it's the other way around.

I remember the first time I pitched to "Bad" Henry Aaron in the big leagues. He was my idol since I was maybe nine years old, and I still have enormous respect for him as a total professional. It was the day I described earlier, in which I got a single, two doubles, and stole a base. It was the day I got on Aaron's list with his 451st home run. It was also the day I got him on my list by striking him out—and thereby hangs the tale.

When he came to bat the first time I could hardly bear it. There I was facing the man I'd fantasized about for so long, pitching to him when I threw a rubber ball against the chimney of my home. I had to turn away from him and look toward center field to clear my head. Still I could see his mannerisms, the way he put his batting helmet on with both hands, the way he tossed away the weighted bat, the way he set himself in the batter's box.

On the third pitch he hit an inside fastball into a double play. I was throwing a good fastball that day, and Aaron's second time up I threw three fastballs past him. That impressed me. Apparently it impressed him, too.

The third time up, I remembered how well I did with the fastball, and this time Aaron cracked it 400 feet for a home run. Pitchers aren't the only ones who think.

When the good hitters think, the least you can do is try to keep it an even match.

Some of what is known as being a smart pitcher is really the ability to throw the ball where you want it. That's control. The rest of being a smart pitcher is in knowing what to throw and where to throw it. The basic rule is to throw the hitter something he doesn't expect to a place he doesn't expect it.

That's like saying: If the stock goes up, buy it; if it doesn't go up, don't buy it.

The fundamental pitching pattern is that a fastball up and in sets up a curve low and outside—also the curve low and away sets up the fastball high and inside. Then you get into the double-think of the operation: If you throw a fastball up and in and the hitter then expects the curve low and away, what you've set him up for is another fastball up and in.

The concept is to confuse the hitter and break his timing. You mustn't permit your pitching to fall into a pattern the hitter can anticipate.

Trying to out think the hitter is probably the most fun you can have pitching—when he doesn't guess right.

There's one more vital concept to understand: Keep the ball down. There are very few good hitters who prefer the ball below their waist. The explanation is simple. Have someone take a baseball and hold it out in front of you chest high; notice how much of the hitting face of the ball you see. Then have him hold it knee high. How much less do you see then of the area the hitter wants to hit with the bat? That's what you want to give him.

103

The exception is the overpowering fastball that jumps over the hitter's bat. But then, that kind of power gives the pitcher permission for an exception to a lot of things.

PLACEMENT

Make this chart for yourself to help you determine where your pitches work best. Take a piece of school paper and draw an imaginary strike zone (as on the diagram) as you face it from the mound. Draw several. Record the way you pitched to the hitters and how it worked out. You'll soon find out where your pitches work best and worst.

Some pitchers use one placement for right-handed hitters and another for lefties. I find that, with a few exceptions, my placement stays the same for either hitter. I know that my curveball is most effective low and outside to a right-handed hitter and naturally low and inside to a lefty. I have much better control of the ball and better movement in those areas.

Rising Fastball. You want that pitch on the top edge of the strike zone so the hitter swings under it. You also want it in on the hands so he has the least time to get his bat around.

To hit the inside fastball the hitter must be very quick with the bat. If he anticipates and swings too soon, he pulls it foul. If he's too slow he hits the ball on the handle and breaks his bat. The area is sometimes known as the batter's "kitchen." When you snap his bat, you can say, "I got in his kitchen and broke his dishes."

If you miss with the pitch, you want to miss inside. If you get the ball too far over the plate, that territory belongs to the hitter.

This is my concept of working every hitter as if he were right-handed. Instead of trying to jam a left-handed hitter with a pitch on the handle, often I'll try to make him hit it off the end of the bat. He can't do much damage with that. Besides, often a

104

right-hander's fastball will tail away from a left-handed hitter and make the outside pitch that much more difficult for him.

If you're left-handed, reverse that idea.

The most devastating pitch is that rising fastball at the knees. The ball is coming low, where the hitter can't see much of it, and it elevates into the strike zone. Nobody can hit that pitch. Also almost nobody can throw it. I can throw it maybe two or three games a year, on those days when I feel awfully strong.

A smart pitcher with a good rising fastball can go up the "ladder" with it. He throws the first one chest high, the next armpit high, and the third just above the strike zone. The hitters strike out on those or pop them up.

Sinking Fastball. That's down and in to righties and down and away to lefties. Hopefully you get the lefties to go for this one and hit it into a double play.

Curveball. The pitching area is much more limited for a curveball than for a fastball. You can get away with fewer mistakes. The curveball is low. That's all. To a right-handed hitter I'll always try to throw it for the low-outside corner. Sometimes I'll try to make it break out of the strike zone and make the batter chase a pitch he can hardly reach. That kind of pitch is most effective when you have two strikes on the batter, and he can't take a chance of being called out on strikes.

It's also a good pitch after you've just thrown a fastball high and inside. Often the hitter will back away from the plate just a bit after a high-inside pitch, and consequently he won't be able to get a good swing at a low-outside pitch.

Sometimes a curveball is very effective to a left-handed hitter when it's thrown off the plate outside, and it breaks enough to catch the corner after the hitter has decided to take it.

The movement of your curveball will vary from day to day. When you're warming up, don't expect it to be exactly the same pitch you threw the last time you pitched. Pay attention to how the ball is breaking, and guide yourself from that. In general, I aim

105

my curve at the waist of a right-handed batter and expect it to break from there. But when I'm throwing particularly well and my concentration is just right, I won't aim there at all. I think I'm going to throw my curve to a particular spot—and I throw it there. Nothing to it.

Of course, I've learned my curve quite well by now. And those are on the good days. I sometimes throw the curveball higher than I intend, which is known as a hanging curve. Batting averages get fat on hanging curves.

Slider. Your target area for the slider is much the same as for the curve, although you can come up a little higher with the slider. Basically, you want it low. To a left-handed hitter, you can throw it in on his hands. If the pitch looks like a fastball and the hitter reacts as if he saw a fastball—and then the ball moves in on him the result is often a broken bat. Sometimes the slider is thrown to break over the outside corner to a left-hander, but the maximum advantage is made of that pitch when it's in tight to a lefty.

The fastball in combination with the slider is an effective tool. Think of throwing a slider that looks like a fastball and breaks away from the hitter, followed by a fastball that looks the same as the pitch before. The hitter begins to lean in and finds the pitch doesn't break. The next pitch, when he's leery, is the curve on the corner low and outside. And then you can reverse the sequence.

Change-up. Always throw the change-up low, as we discussed before. But there are other rules involving the change that are rules of good sense.

Don't make your first pitch to a hitter a change. The purpose of the change is to break a hitter's timing, and it's relative to the pitch you threw before as well as the pitch to follow. Let a hitter see a fastball or a curve to get a sense of timing before you let him see your change. If he hasn't seen the fastball, he may not know this one is the change and think it's just a lousy fastball. That's the one he hits a mile.

When Brent Strom was called up from the minor leagues to pitch for the Mets at the end of one season, the first pitch he ever threw to Johnny Bench was a change. Bang! Bench hit a home run. I tried to explain to Strom in the dugout after the inning that you have to have a comparison to something to make the change useful.

Don't give weak hitters a slow pitch. The bad hitters aren't fooled by the change; in fact they're encouraged by it. Overpower those hitters. Largely they're such poor hitters that the change is just what they want.

READ THE HITTER

There are times you can merely look at a hitter and read his mind. You know by the way he holds his hands back and twists his body that he's trying to hit to the opposite field. You can see when he's trying to pull by leaning his body. You can see when he's looking for a fastball. It's like there's a big neon sign.

There are two ways to make that information work for you. If he's looking for an outside pitch, you can throw him inside pitches and defeat his plan. Or you can throw him outside pitches that are a little farther outside than he wants. If he goes for them, he's your pal.

The majority of power hitters want to pull the ball and prefer an inside pitch to pull. Except for Richie Allen. He wants to hit through the middle, past where I'm standing. Groan. I did not weep when he was traded to the American League. Nor did the rest of the National League.

During one game I was pitching to the late Roberto Clemente, and he was clearly looking to hit to the opposite field, as he often did. He wanted that curveball breaking away from him so he could drive it into right field and score the runner on second.

I was throwing very hard that day, and I threw a fastball past him on the first pitch. I thought, "A fastball down the pipe with a man on second, and he took it? The son of a gun must be looking for a breaking ball." I threw another fastball over the plate away, and he took it.

107

I thought, "He really does want a breaking ball. Okay, I'll make him think a curve is coming." Duffy Dyer gave me a sign for a fastball; I shook it off, even though it was the pitch I wanted to throw, and the pitch Duffy knew was right for the situation. He called for a curve, and I shook it off; a slider, and I shook it off. Then Duffy was back to the fastball. We had Clemente dead.

I started the windup. His hands were going, his legs were going, and he was saying, "Here comes that breaking ball." The fastball was right under his chin as he lunged. He·was going to swing anyhow, but his bat was a foot behind the pitch.

The last thing he expected was another fastball. You rarely want to give a hitter two pitches in a row that are the same speed, much less three, and Clemente knew it. Unless it's an overpowering fastball. The exception is that most hitters don't expect a change to be followed by another change—or let you know that they're looking for a fastball to follow a curve. Your job is to throw them what they don't expect.

There are hitters you absolutely don't want to see the same pitch twice in a row. Those are the hitters who don't guess at what's coming. They are there to hit whatever is coming. You throw one curveball, then another, and the sense of timing and recognition is fresh in their minds: They're very dangerous. Joe Torre is one of those, Rusty Staub is another. They're controlled, intelligent hitters.

GETTING AN OUT

There are times when you want the ball hit in the air, and times when it's just what you don't want. With runners on first and third and one out, you want the batter to hit a double-play ball on the ground, not a sacrifice fly. With a runner on second and none out, you don't want the hitter to ground to the right side to advance the runner to third.

Hitters have individual swings, but predominantly you'll get ground balls with a curve low and outside or a fastball low and inside. If the fastball is fast enough and close enough, the hitter won't get the good part of his bat around quick enough; he'll hit weakly on the ground. On the curveball, as the bat comes down the ball is moving down, and it strikes the lower part of the bat.

When you want a hitter to pop up—when you don't want a lot of grounders, the only pitch is the riding fastball. The ball is moving up; the hitter swings under it.

That's the pitch the hitters pop up—that or the hanging curve, if you're lucky. It's always a good idea to be lucky, too.

109

9

Control of the Game

Luck is a beautiful thing to have on your side, but Casey Stengel gave us a bit of philosophy on the subject that should endure forever. To players who blamed their own inadequacies or unwillingness to work hard enough on bad luck, Stengel said:

"Bad luck, your ear; you'll have bad luck all your life. You make your own luck."

Branch Rickey, a more erudite man, said: "Luck is the residue of design."

It all means, if you work hard and do your own job well, you'll be able to take advantage of your luck. What difference does it make if the catcher drops a foul ball with a runner on third if the batter doesn't get a hit on his second life?

Gary Gentry was forever struggling with his own temper when he was on the Mets. If the umpire called "ball" on a pitch Gentry thought was a strike, it would enrage him. Gentry would still be thinking about the call on the last pitch when he was throwing the next pitch. That was the vulnerable one hit.

One of the lowest points in my major league career came because my mind wasn't where it should have been. It was in 1970, when we were trying to get ourselves back on the track of the great 1969 championship season. We had a one-run lead with one out in the last of the ninth inning at Atlanta, and the Braves had the tying run on third.

We had two strikes on Bob Tillman, and I knew if I threw a

Some days your best just isn't good enough. You wait for the new pitcher to relieve you, then you walk off with your head down—to think about what it was you didn't do right.
(Newsday photo)

fastball high and inside he was struck out—no question about it. I had already recorded the strikeout in my mind and was thinking about how to pitch to the hitter on deck, Felix Millan. I was so wrapped up in my thoughts that I never even read the sign from Jerry Grote calling for a curve.

I threw the fastball right where I wanted it. Unfortunately, Grote shifted to the outside corner for the curve that never came. The pitch was strike three, but the ball sailed over Grote's mitt, back to the backstop. I was so dumbfounded by the whole thing that I was late covering the plate and couldn't handle Grote's throw on the runner coming home.

111

The tying run scored, and we eventually lost in extra innings. A very punishing lesson.

It's your responsibility to know the game and to stay in the game. Know the rule book. Keep a copy in the locker room and read a couple of pages at a time until you know what's in it. Make the rules of the game work for you, not against you.

Late in the 1969 season, as we were closing in on first place, we went into the ninth inning at Los Angeles trailing the Dodgers by one run. With one out in the top of the ninth, Gil Hodges sent Rod Gaspar to the plate as a pinch hitter. Gaspar, who was often used as a defensive outfielder, made the second out. When the next batter made the third out, the game was over. The Dodgers won; we lost.

As the Mets in the dugout stood up to leave for the clubhouse, Gaspar looked at the manager. "Gil," he said, "you want me to go to left field?"

Hodges stared at Gaspar for just a moment. Not much longer. "Yeah," the manager said. "You go to left."

Rod took two steps out of the dugout and suddenly realized the Dodgers were coming off, and he was the only Met going on the field. He saw that the game was over, that he had lost track of it. He was embarrassed.

I don't think anybody stayed in the game any closer than Gaspar for the rest of the season.

Staying in the game for the pitcher means being aware of things like a batter's characteristics. I know that Matty Alou likes to beat the ball on the ground to the third-base side. That means I have to try to make him pull, which he doesn't want to do. On some occasions, though, he'll crowd the plate, on others he'll lay back. It's the pitcher's job to see that.

It's the pitcher's job to understand what the game is all about, too. When a runner is on second base with none out, the batter should be trying to hit the ball on the ground to the right side to get the runner to third. The pitcher should be trying to defeat that.

If you keep your head in the game, even when you aren't playing, your observations might help you, or they can be passed on to help a teammate.
(Newsday photo)

When a sacrifice fly will score a run from third, you want to make the batter hit on the ground.

When there's a runner on second base and the batter singles to the outfield, expect a throw to come to the plate and be prepared to back up the plate.

Learn to work with a catcher. It's very simple: Two heads are better than one. The catcher and pitcher working together can remember more about hitters and have better control of a situation.

Before a game you should sit down and discuss the hitters and what you plan to throw. As the game goes on, you should be in communication with the catcher about what each pitch is doing. Perhaps he can tell you to lay off the slider today and make more use of the curve because it's working so well.

The catcher gives the signals for each pitch. Usually they're simple. One finger for a fastball, two for a curve, three for a slider, four for a change. A fist is generally used to call for a pitchout when the catcher thinks a runner may be stealing.

As you play in higher levels of baseball, the signs can get more complicated to prevent the other team from reading them. Remember, when there's a runner on second base, he's looking in at the same fingers as the pitcher.

Then the pitcher and catcher use an indicator system. For example: If the catcher rubs his bare hand across his chest protector, the second signal will be the intended pitch; a rub on the shinguard will make it the first pitch.

That's communication. The catcher should know what the pitcher is going to throw. But the pitcher has the responsibility of shaking off a pitch he doesn't think he should throw.

In my first season in the major leagues Jerry Grote used to be disturbed when he caught me, and I shook off his signals. One day he came out to the mound—angry—and asked, "Who do you think is calling this game?"

I said, "I am. I'm the last one who touches the ball before it gets to the plate. I want to throw what I think is right."

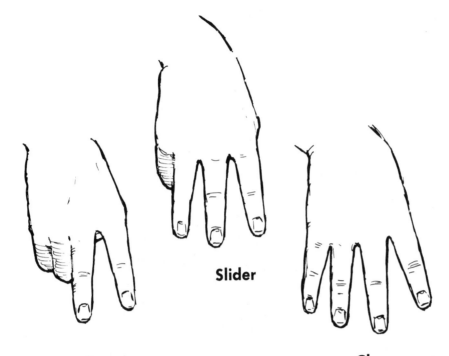

Slider

Curve

Change-up

Fastball

Pitchout

The simplest signals are: One finger for a fastball, two for a curve, three for a slider, four for a change-up, and a fist for a pitchout.

115

The runner on second can see the signs, too, have to throw him off. When the catcher ma first signal one finger, he might mean the firs signal after that one is the pitch he wants; an then he will give a few more signals as a deco

Jerry conceded, after he got over his surprise. "Well, I guess you are."

Once you and the catcher work together you should get to know how each other thinks. Now I rarely have to shake off Grote's signals. Often I shake off a pitch I want to throw in order to confuse the batter and wait until the catcher gives the signal the second time. Often you can disturb a hitter by making him wait.

Sometimes you need to put your head together with the catcher's for a suggestion—or whatever. You may want to know what's the matter with what you're throwing. Sometimes you'll just want to take a breather. And sometimes the catcher will insist on you pausing for a moment by coming out to the mound. Perhaps you're rushing your motion or trying to overthrow.

Sometimes what the catcher has to say is important. Sometimes it isn't. Sometimes it doesn't make any difference if he says anything or not.

There used to be a catcher with the Mets named Choo Choo Coleman, who had caught in the Phillies organization. There he caught a no-hitter pitched by one Clarence Nottingham Churn. When Chuck Churn was asked who was the most difficult man to pitch to, he replied: "Coleman."

Anyhow, Coleman was catching at Jacksonville the year I was there, and one day I went through a spell of wildness.

Choo Choo came to the mound and talked to me for what seemed like a long time, maybe a minute and a half—two minutes. I'm sure I didn't understand a thing he said, but I nodded as he spoke; then he went back behind the plate. Sure enough, as soon as I began pitching again I had command of my stuff as if Choo Choo had said magic words.

Sometimes it's just a breather you need on the mound, and sometimes it's a change of thinking that the catcher can give you.

ADVANCED PLAY

You really can't begin to imagine how complicated pitching and baseball can be until you get to its highest level.

The pickoff at second base is one of the more sophisticated plays we use. It's not a lot different from a second-base pickoff used in high school, but the way it's executed can be so fine when it's done by men who've practiced for years. Sometimes the catcher calls the play; sometimes the infielder, and sometimes the coach.

The major rule on this is the same as throwing to any base: Make a good throw. Throw over the top of the bag about knee high. Have a simple signal with the shortstop and second baseman, something that looks natural but isn't a gesture you'd make accidentally. Wipe your hand on your leg, or adjust your belt. And the infielder covering the base would give a countersign that he understood, perhaps tugging at his cap.

You go into your stretch position and look back toward second base. As soon as you turn your head and look toward the plate, the count begins: 1,001, 1,002.

At 1,002, the infielder breaks behind the runner for the bag. On 1,003, you turn and make your good throw to the base.

Little Black Book. It pays to keep a notebook on everything you do on the mound. It becomes more important when you pitch against the same hitters several times in a season. Then you record which pitches you used to get a hitter out and which ones he hit. You try to remember all that history each time you face a batter.

You can use that information even if you play the same school only twice in a season. If a batter has two hits on curveballs his first two times up, you wouldn't want to give him a good curveball the third time up, would you? Then why not remember from March until May that the second baseman for Springfield hits curveballs.

You can also see your own pattern clearly. If you get hit on your slider and not on your curve, you can see it on paper and understand that the slider needs more work and not to throw it in a dangerous situation.

There are things you do when you have a big lead that you don't do in a close game. When you have a four- or five-run lead in the late innings, you don't want to walk anybody. That's the most foolish thing you can do when the best chance a batted ball has of being a hit is four in ten. With a lead, you throw strikes. Throw your good stuff, but concentrate on making the hitters swing at the ball. You don't have to throw every pitch on the corner.

Also, if you're in a situation like pitching the first game of a playoff and have to face the same team three days later, keep it in mind. If you have that good lead, you can throw pitches to hitters they might never see in a close game.

These are things you see shining in the bright light at the end of the long tunnel. They are some of the reward for experimenting, learning, thinking, and working. They are the end of the equation that adds hard work, dedication, concentration, and God-given talent and producing a good ballplayer.

I'm reminded of a day when I was in boot camp in the Marine Corps, my hair still hardly longer than fuzz, but I had worked when the Marine Corps told me to work and learned what I had to learn. All the screaming, mental punishment, and plain sweat were still with me, but I was winning my game with the Corps.

After one routine exhausting day we were at dinner, and I had a perfectly dreadful piece of blueberry pie on my tray. I offered it across the table to an old friend, and it must have been a joke, because I surely knew he wouldn't eat it either. We must have giggled, or the drill instructor must have heard my offer. Anyway, it set off an explosion.

All the while the Marine Corps had been hounding us to do it faster and do it quieter—whatever it was we were doing. "Seaver!" the drill instructor screamed. "Is that you talking down there?" I kept on eating.

"Seaver! Is that you?" The DI jumped up onto the table. The

table must have been forty feet long with trainees and their trays on either side all the way. The DI ran down the middle of the table, stepping into trays and splattering food and bits of blueberry pie all over the place in his rage to get to me.

"What the hell are you talking about, Seaver?" he screamed and began kicking his toe into my ribs.

I knew then what the Marine Corps and I had made out of my body. My muscles were as hard as they've ever been in my life, as hard as could be. "Get that damned food in your mouth and chew it later," the DI screamed. All the while he was kicking me as hard as he could from the tabletop. And I had tears running down my cheeks to keep from laughing. He couldn't hurt me. I was too well-prepared.

Maybe that's the point. The hitters have their days against the best of pitchers. They'll get you too, no matter how hard you work. Sometimes.

But there will be those days when you're ready. You've done your running, and your legs are strong. Your concentration is just right, and it seems you can will a curveball over the low outside corner. You can stand out there on the mound, the hitters trying as hard as they can, and behind your most earnest look you can laugh at the whole world.

It isn't even the fact of getting the hitters out. It's more that you've set your own standards—you've set them high, and you're meeting them. That's the time being a pitcher pays the greatest reward any athlete can ask.

Sometimes I'm happy, especially after a one-hitter
against the Padres. We beat them 2-0. *(AP photo)*

A special ball for the trophy case and for the photographers. On the last day of the 1971 season I set the National League strikeout record, won my twentieth game and wound up with the lowest earned-run average in the league. *(AP photo)*

You don't expect to win many games by hitting a home
run yourself, but they are delightful moments. I hit
one in Cincinnati in 1972, and we won the game 2-1.
There were the big smiles, the handshakes and that
Met banner waving in the sea of Cincinnati fans.
(UPI photo)

10

The Future Lies Ahead

Let's be realistic about the whole thing. How many boys are there playing baseball? How many of them are pitchers? They all have that dream of pitching in the big leagues, of winning twenty games against the best.

How many pitchers are there in the big leagues? Figure ten on a team and twenty-four big-league teams. That's two hundred and forty pitchers realizing the dream at any one time.

The odds are very great. I don't mean to kill the dream, but the odds say you won't make it.

The dream is a wonderful thing. It took years for me to realize I was living what I'd always dreamed. But it can't be the only thing in your life.

There are a lot of boys who face a decision each year at the time of high school graduation. Some of them chose to take their chance in the minor leagues. Some of them chose to go on to college, perhaps play ball there and continue to fuel that dream.

Not many of either will ever make it. The ones who begin an education will have an advantage. I had two years of college before I signed a contract. With two years completed, it's not so difficult to finish the last two years of college. It's awfully hard to do four years of college, one semester at a time in the offseason. I admire anyone who can do it. Your education will stay with you forever, long after your last fastball has faded.

The others never play anything more professional than a sandlot game that pays off in Cokes. The reward for them is the fun of playing for one team that beats another team—or even for playing for the losing team, if they've tried their best.

And that's fine, too. They're welcome to be pitchers.